GEORGES BIZET

From a photograph by Et. Carjat & Cie

BIZET

GEORGES BIZET

HIS LIFE AND WORKS

BY

DOUGLAS CHARLES PARKER

Select Bibliographies Reprint Series

 BOOKS FOR LIBRARIES PRESS

FREEPORT, NEW YORK

First Published 1926
Reprinted 1969

780.92
B625p

STANDARD BOOK NUMBER:
8369-5054-2

LIBRARY OF CONGRESS CATALOG CARD NUMBER:
73-94280

PRINTED IN THE UNITED STATES OF AMERICA

CONTENTS

CONTENTS—(*Continued*)

GEORGES BIZET

CHAPTER I

Birth—First Lessons—Conservatoire—His Teachers—Prix de Rome—Sojourn in Italy—Return to Paris—Death of his Mother—Creative Activity—Marriage—Symphonic Ambitions—Franco-Prussian War—Djamileh—L'Arlésienne—Carmen.

ALEXANDRE CÉSAR LÉOPOLD (commonly called Georges [1]) Bizet was born in Paris on the 25th of October, 1838. Like many another child, he breathed a musical atmosphere from the date of his birth. His father was a teacher of singing, and a sister of his mother, Madame Delsarte, who in her time had carried off the first piano prize at the Paris Conservatoire, enjoyed a considerable reputation as a brilliant executant. It was not long before the child gave positive proof of an alert intelligence, and a strong love of music. At the age of four his interest in the art had become so manifest that his mother taught him the notes, as well as the letters of the alphabet. She found him a pupil both apt and eager to learn, and his progress was so rapid that it might well have astonished the casual visitor to the Bizet household.

[1] The name bestowed upon him by his godfather.

I

The routine thus early established appears to have run its course for several years. The fond mother continued to impart knowledge to the slender, vivacious, and bright-minded child. The child, on his part, looked forward to his music lessons with an eagerness to which most children are total strangers. Even these did not satisfy him. He would leave his games in order to listen at the door when his father was engaged with pupils. Astonished, no doubt, at the ease with which his son learnt, and having observed how much music meant to him, the father determined to take the precocious youth in hand. Convinced as he was of the aptitudes of his ambitious child, a closer knowledge only tended to increase his amazement. With a capacity worthy of one far beyond his years went an extraordinary memory. One day, it is recorded, Georges executed a difficult singing exercise with an ease and assurance that struck the father as unusual. On looking up, Bizet *père* discovered that the student had discarded the music-book and was performing a treacherous task from memory.

Before many months had run their course the father realised that, if Georges were to advance further in his art, he must be placed in other hands. The Conservatoire seemed, naturally, to be the place best fitted to satisfy the needs of the situation. There remained one formidable obstacle— the age of the youthful aspirant for musical honours. While realising this, the father determined to find out whether the obstacle could not, by hook or crook, be overcome. In this he was, no doubt, fortified by a deep-rooted belief in his son's capacity, which seemed sufficiently remarkable to justify a departure from common practice. He sought out an old friend, Alizard, who held a post at the Opéra. After talking over the matter, the two friends decided upon the line they would take up. They would approach Meifred, one of the members of the Committee of Studies.

This gentleman was at first sceptical. Persons of his rank and station are inclined to be so. There are so many wonderful children, whose mothers and fathers dote upon them and interpret their smallest actions as promises of future immortality. The world regards them with a different eye, and Meifred, for the moment, was the world. 'Another fond father !' he may have thought to himself. But, like a practical man, he came to the point quickly by inquiring what the stripling knew. This pleased the father. He could certainly demonstrate that the boy was far from being a dullard, which he did by inviting Meifred to go to the piano, strike a few chords, and ask his son to name them. Without hesitation, Georges named the chords and the intervals. He immediately won the regard of Meifred, who, finding it impossible to conceal his surprise, declared that a student so apt would surely win a place at the Institute.

The way was clear. A letter signed by Auber,

at that time director of the Conservatoire, requested Monsieur Bizet to present himself on the 12th of October, 1848, at 11.30 a.m., and bring with him his certificates of birth and vaccination. That the recipient carried out the instructions to the letter need not be doubted. The first preliminary stage had been completed ; the second, more fruitful and impressive, was about to begin.

When Bizet entered the Conservatoire he had not yet celebrated the tenth anniversary of his birth. As it happened, the staff of that institution grappled with as many students as could properly be accommodated within its walls. Until a place could be found for him, the newcomer attended the piano class of Marmontel, of which he soon became an ornament. Marmontel was at once impressed by the personality of his new pupil. In his volume, *Symphonistes et Virtuoses*, he tells us that Bizet cared little for the sensational, but dwelt upon that which was well written. Youth is generally a period of fierce likes and dislikes, which are shouted from the housetops for all the world to hear. It is this candour, this dogmatism, so often naïve, this confidence of being right, even in the presence of minds mature and experienced, which lend to youth one of its greatest charms. Like most musicians of a tender age, Bizet had his decided preferences. Marmontel was not the man to dismiss these with the bland smile of superiority.

4

He obeyed a sound instinct, which told him that, in order to teach a subject, one must have knowledge of more than that subject ; one must fully understand the individual to whom the subject is being taught. And so, instead of poohpoohing the young fellow, as a martinet or doctrinaire would have done, he frankly encouraged Bizet to give the reasons for his preferences. By this method, he confessed, one is able to guide and form the taste of students.

Needless to say, the work of Marmontel did not absorb all Bizet's energies. In the organ class of Benoist he speedily distinguished himself. He loved the organ and revelled in the great music written for it.

So much for the practical side ; on the theoretical, Bizet was far from idle. Marmontel recounts how Zimmermann came to him one day, asking the names of any pupils who wished to study counterpoint, and adds that among those which he gave his colleague was the name of Bizet. Reports regarding the cleverness of Bizet had, as a matter of fact, reached the quick ear of the old contrapuntist. Naturally, he wished to make the acquaintance of so promising a musician. The anxiety he thus betrayed was thoroughly characteristic of Zimmermann. For over thirty years he had laboured with a zeal, devotion, and disinterestedness worthy of his high calling. At the period of which I speak, he was no longer a young man, and, feeling the burden of his years, sought to lighten his labours. This did not prevent his taking under his wing several students to whom he felt particularly attracted.

Zimmermann deservedly occupies a prominent position among the musical pedagogues of France. Born in 1785, he had studied with an exacting taskmaster, Cherubini himself. At the age of twenty-six he accepted a subordinate position at the Conservatoire. From that time onwards his life was spent in class rooms. His pupils were his first thought ; their welfare was that which lay closest to his heart. Some men find the call of the sea irresistible. The sound of trumpet and drum stirs others to the very depths of their being, and inspires them to feats of valour. Far lands, with their riotous colours and intoxicating perfumes, throw a glamour upon restless, imaginative minds. But there are joys and triumphs far removed from these, of which the world takes little heed. Zimmermann tasted their sweetness. Destiny did not mark him out for spectacular achievement. He was happy in the work he found ready to his hand. He asked for nothing save the pleasure to be derived from instruction. His successes were successes once removed— those of his pupils. He had patience and industry, as well as the divine gift of self-abnegation.

Good fortune smiled on Bizet when the professor met him. Zimmermann quickly gauged the worth of his friend, rejoiced in the brightness of his intelligence, and in the charm of his personality. Inevitably, he found time to instruct one so apt and willing to learn. That Bizet owed much to Zimmermann can scarcely be doubted. His new teacher had enjoyed a wide and varied experience ; he had himself learnt counterpoint from Cherubini, an indubitable master of that subject ; he had an admirable faculty for imparting knowledge. It will be granted that what the student learned from a professor so well equipped permitted him to make the fullest use of the lessons he was to receive from Halévy subsequently.

Unfortunately, Zimmermann's health left much to be desired. Years of conscientious toil had left their mark upon him. For help he looked to one of the most prominent of the young musicians to be found in France, Charles Gounod. At this time, consequently, there first came into contact two musicians, each of whom was destined to bequeath to the world an immensely popular operatic score, and write a page upon the history of French dramatic art.

After Zimmermann's death, which occurred in 1853, Bizet continued to pursue his studies sedulously with Halévy. For over twenty years Halévy had appeared before the opera-going public. *La Juive*, which brought him fame in 1835, was followed by a considerable number of operas that came in quick succession. But, industriously as he drove his pen, he managed to find time for professional work. In 1833 he had been appointed professor of counterpoint and fugue, in 1840 professor of composition. Through his hands passed several of the brightest representatives of the younger generation, of whom Gounod, Bizet, Lecocq and Victor Massé are, perhaps, the best known to-day. None of them, however, won a higher place in his esteem than the subject of these lines. Like Marmontel and Zimmermann, he received Bizet with a warmth indicative of his sincere admiration.

As for Halévy himself in the rôle of professor, let it be said that he boasted a sound technical knowledge and a rich practical experience. Not for nothing had he wrestled with the intricacies of composition under the eagle eye of Cherubini ; and he had added liberally to the repertoire of the stages of Paris. A man who could point to such accomplishment was likely to impress an ambitious youth at his most impressionable age, and we need not be astonished that the admiration of the master was matched by that of the pupil.

Bizet, then, was fortunate in his professors. Each in turn had taken a genuine interest in him, because each felt that he was no ordinary student. Time yielded ample justification for this unanimous verdict. Bizet's career wanted nothing of academic brilliance. In these days wise people do not attach undue significance to the winning of prizes. The boy who sits at the top of the class is not invariably the boy who succeeds in later life. Every-day experience goes to prove that some minds are like a rocket. They astonish by reason of their rise and flash, but their mobility and incandescence do not last for long. So far from fulfilling early promises, many students pay for them by years devoted to average, if not mediocre, performances. And there exist others whose happy knack of carrying off distinctions is purchased by an apparent inability to do anything else. Bizet must have had this happy knack, with the good qualities it implies—an ability to do oneself justice at the right moment, and a mastery over both nerves and faculties. But it ought to be added that he had something more, something of greater value both for himself and for his art, as his subsequent career showed. His record, I have said, was excellent. In 1849 he took a *prix de Solfège* ; in 1851 the second prize for piano ; in 1852 the first prize for piano ; in 1854 the second prizes for fugue and for organ, and in 1855 the first prizes for fugue and for organ.

Having achieved so much, he might reasonably try his strength in the supreme contest, that for the *prix de Rome*. He first entered the lists in 1856, when the subject set was a cantata entitled *David*, the book of which bore the name of Gaston d'Albano. After considerable deliberation, the judges decided that they could not award a first grand prize. Bizet, nevertheless, emerged at the top of the poll with a second grand prize. According to Pigot, the biographer, the jury arrived at this decision in view of Bizet's age, and voiced the opinion that an additional year with Halévy would render more flexible the precocious talent of the young master. So the young master went back to work. Day followed day, week followed week, until at length the time again arrived when it would be necessary for him to put his best foot forward and show of what stuff he was made. In 1857, he, for the second time, challenged his right to the highest award within the reach of a French music student. But, before saying more about this matter, I must turn back the hands of the clock in order to touch upon one or two of his earliest ventures into the great world of music.

Rossini, we are told, fled the schoolroom as soon as he realised that poor old Mattei credited him with enough knowledge to write operas. The impetuous Italian worked at first on an irreducible minimum. What had he to do with a two-power standard, with that margin of strength and resource to be called into play on some hypothetical occasion ? The higher reaches to be attained by those who had mastered the strict style he left lightheartedly to others. Man lives but once, and youth fades like a damask rose. The harvest of the hour is very pleasant, the call of the cheerful footlights very strong. Wise in his day and generation is he who, taking the tide at the flood, floats on the bosom of the waters to success. This was the philosophy of Rossini's nonage ; a philosophy which, as we shall discover, Ambroise

Thomas, speaking *ex cathedrâ*, would have condemned in no measured terms.

One dwells upon such things, because the passing from the class-room to the theatre or concert hall forms one of the most absorbing, if also one of the most dangerous, incidents in a composer's odyssey. In the passing the composer changes masters. Leaving a teacher, who, wisely or unwisely, wields a blue pencil, the ear-tickler falls under the domination of the public ; the artist troubled with a conscience recognises in himself the ultimate arbiter. Either must, in the nature of the case, be aware of a change in atmosphere, in values, and in status. There are cliques and foibles, fashions and crotchets both inside and outside conservatoire doors. Yet these are not the same cliques and foibles, fashions and crotchets. Questions that agitate enthusiastic students often leave undisturbed the serenity of the man in the street and of the man in the theatre. That which a professor in his Olympic moments praises as good or denounces as bad is not likely to be exactly what the heterogeneous and myriad-minded mass, which we call the public, will praise as good or denounce as bad. Moreover, the composer now stands upon his own legs. He has only himself to look to in the last resort, though it should be said, if such unfashionable view be permitted, that he can learn much from the past ; the past which has so many lessons for him that, did he live for three score years and ten, he could not learn them all. His instructors sought to nourish and develop his endowment by discipline, and by an enlargement and strengthening of his acquirements. When he begins his professional career he must impose a discipline upon himself, as Beethoven did ; he must decide for himself what is right and what is wrong ; he must, in a word, satisfy his own sense of artistic integrity.

Although their intrinsic value may be small, the early works of composers possess an attraction for the historian. If youthful spirits, conscious of their waxing strength, smash some altars on the road to fame, they stop to burn incense before others. The love for this or that writer betrays itself in a score, which says without eloquence what others have said in the accents of conviction. But the man of inquiring mind will always wish to know what such a score is like, because he longs to satisfy himself as to the direction, length and duration of the composer's journey ; because he desires to institute comparisons ; and because he feels it not unprofitable to test the music in relation to the period and circumstances of its composition, and to the composer's age. What do they know of Verdi who only *Falstaff* know ?

Keeping in mind the ardour of Bizet's temperament, and the deep-seated desire to justify himself as musician which he so frequently exhibited, one can hardly imagine that he did not look forward to the hour when he would have a chance to invite the attention of the public. In his dreams he must often have lived through that hour, so momentous and so glorious to those conscious of their strength. An observation by Pigot hints that Bizet did not show indecent haste. Pigot says that Halévy desired his pupil to enter for the *prix de Rome* earlier than 1856, the year of his first entry. From this, one infers that Bizet placed great stress upon Halévy's tuition, that he enjoyed his years of pupilage immensely, or that he recognised the safety of slow travel.

Whether Bizet's theatrical début was made in 1854 or 1857 is a point on which opinions are not unanimous. In his interesting book entitled *Musiciens français d'Aujourd'hui*, Octave Séré remarks that it is a fact generally ignored that the composer's début belongs to the year 1854, when, with Philippe Gille, author of the libretto, he produced at Baden an operetta in one act, entitled *La Prêtresse*. Not having heard of this operetta, I made inquiries in a quarter from which light should have been forthcoming. As a result, I have been informed, in words which do not allow of misinterpretation, that Bizet at no time collaborated with Philippe Gille, and my informant, who had not heard of *La Prêtresse*, declared that such an operetta never existed.

A little more light can be thrown upon *Docteur Miracle*. Never at a loss for an idea, Offenbach announced a competition calculated to cause composers to shun delights, and shut themselves in their rooms with ink, music-paper, and the

inevitable " book." Competitors had to set a
libretto written by Léon Battu and Ludovic
Halévy, which bore the Hoffmannesque title
just mentioned. The winning operetta was to be
presented at the Bouffes Parisiens. Of course, the
bait tempted. Apart from the measure of renown
to be gained, intending competitors had in mind
the possibility, if not the probability, of actual
performance. An alluring bait this ; for the
writing of an opera is sometimes as nothing compared with the hawking, cajoling, and pleading to
be gone through before someone takes it up.
Bizet attacked the work, finding in it at once an
outlet for his ideas and a contrast to his academic
studies. Curiously enough, he tied for the first
place with a musician who had sat beside him in
Halévy's class—Lecocq. Bizet wrote this score
quickly ; it ran off the very point of his pen.
But I regard it as a distinct mark in his favour that
he emerged so successfully, for in works of this
class Lecocq was in his element, as a long and
enormously successful career proved later. Two
works having been placed on the same level, they
had both to be performed in terms of the conditions. Whether what happened at the Bouffes
Parisiens is absolutely unique in operatic history I
know not ; it is remarkable enough to merit
notice. Two operettas based on the same libretto
were played alternately. The *première* of Lecocq's
version took place on the 8th of April, 1857, that
of Bizet's the following night. The score of the

latter has never been published. For the reason stated above, the inaccessibility of the pieces just mentioned is to be regretted.

Hardly had Bizet put the last touches to *Docteur Miracle* than the *prix de Rome* monopolised his thoughts anew. On this occasion the competitors had to set a lyric scene by Burion, boasting the high-sounding title of *Clovis et Clothilde*. As no first prize had been given in the preceding year, the authorities determined to award two : the winner of the first to be regarded as the laureate of the year, the winner of the second to receive the prize not previously bestowed. A preliminary vote named Charles Colin and Georges Bizet as the successful competitors, in the order mentioned. A subsequent and final vote endorsed this choice, but reversed the order of precedence. Bizet had gained his immediate objective. His years of study had, at last, been crowned with success. In October of this year, 1857, in which so many things had happened to him, his lyric scene was performed in the presence of a brilliant assemblage, and, doubtless, with some of the pomp and effusiveness which Berlioz found characteristic of the function. Report speaks in flattering terms of its reception. " The success," writes Pigot, " was great, very great." By prolonged applause the public ratified the verdict of the Academy.[1]

With this scene, so pleasing to contemplate, a chapter of Bizet's life came to a close. One

[1] Charles Pigot : *Georges Bizet et son Œuvre.*

wonders if his thoughts wandered back to the happy hours when, as a mere infant, he learnt his notes from his mother. One wonders if he did not feel that the real joy which his little triumph brought him lay in something other, and better, than the mere winning of a prize. Had he not justified the words his father addressed to Meifred; had he not justified the faith which Zimmermann and Halévy placed in him ? If he abandoned himself to reflection, he must have looked back at the past and meditated upon the future. The past he could afford to regard with satisfaction. The future stood before him, rich in its promises. It was for him to prove that under his touch the lyre would quiver anew to sweetest song. He had accomplished much, but the very measure of his accomplishment imposed heavy obligations upon him. All life is a battle, and none more so than that of the man who, serving with heart and soul the gods of Art, sweats and labours at his task. Paris had been his home ; the scene of his early dreams and discoveries, his studentship, his academic successes. He was now, for the first time, to part from those dearest to him, a hard wrench for one in whom dwelt a capacity for true friendship. With mingled feelings of regret and pleasurable anticipation, he turned his face towards that smiling land of the South, which holds out its generous arms in affectionate embrace towards the artist.

If the gaining of the *prix de Rome*, as I have

said, closed a chapter of Bizet's artistic life, it also
opened one. The new-crowned laureate might
point to something accomplished, something done.
Yet, if he had in his composition any delicate
feelings about his prestige and good name, he
must have realised that the accomplishment, so
far from earning a night's, or three years', repose
at the expense of the state, invited greater efforts
than he had previously expended on his work.
What lay before him ? For three years the French
Government would pay him annually a certain
sum ; it would give him also allowances for
board, lodging, and travelling expenses. In
return, he would be expected to submit a work
once a year during that period in order to show
what progress he had made. But, it may fairly
be asked, why send the winner to Rome at all ?
What is a musician in his crescent likely to gather
there ? Had we to consider the case of a historian, an archaeologist, or a painter, the question
would not arise. For them the Eternal City
guards a hundred secrets ; every stone is an inspiration ; and countless relics recall, in all their
splendour, the glorious achievements of bygone
ages. Admittedly, the glamours and attractions
of this august centre are of the strongest. What
I am concerned with is their value for a musician.
Are they likely to stimulate him to further endeavour ? The most enthusiastic lover of Rome
will not pretend that it is—it certainly was not in
Bizet's day—a very musical city. When Bizet

had settled in Paris, after his sojourn abroad, Berlioz wrote some lines about him in *Les Debats*. I cannot help thinking that one observation he let fall deserves to be quoted, if only for its delicate irony. " M. Bizet, the laureate of the Institute," said Berlioz, " has made the journey to Rome ; he has come back without having forgotten music." Without having forgotten music—one ponders the words. Perhaps Berlioz remembered the laureate of 1808, Blondeau, of whom it has been said that, though he forgot how to compose, he learnt the Italian language, as a translation of Machiavelli's *The Prince* showed. On this point, Massenet, who carried off the prize in 1863, had no doubt whatever. He expressed himself in favour of the exile. Residence in Rome, he held, might awaken sentiments that would otherwise lie dormant. To be compelled to live far away from the hum of Paris he counted a positive advantage. Tranquillity and solitude compensated for the absence of concerts. But it is not easy, I am convinced, to arrive at the value of the prescribed sojourn in Rome. The extent and quality of its influence defy proof. You cannot say that a man would have been better had he stayed at home, or gone to study elsewhere. All you can say is that on certain temperaments the influence might be expected to be both powerful and beneficial ; because some musical temperaments respond readily to that which, in itself, is not musical. From the North Sea came the

18

storm music of *The Flying Dutchman*. A great
deal of Schumann owes much to Jean Paul, as a
great deal of Liszt found its first impulse in
poetry, painting, and scenery. To men of a like
nature a residence in Rome is likely to stimulate
the imagination and strengthen the soul. This
is an aesthetic advantage, in a real, but also in the
widest, sense, and one pauses to ask if it fully
satisfies the aim in view. The shepherd of Virgil
dwelt among the rocks. Perchance the modest
muses inhabit waste places, that know not the
stir and chatter of the boulevards. If battles
have been won on the playing fields of Eton,
is it not possible that music has been born of the
silence of the Campagna ? From the note of the
pfifferari there is to be learnt that which a symphony orchestra cannot teach. Some men are
able to profit by this lesson, as some men can find
sermons in stones. For others, it will be boredom
and futility unspeakable. But, be it observed,
the exile, to use Massenet's word, did not bring
would-be writers into touch with the music of.
other men ; it did not increase their knowledge
of that which had been written ; nor could it
offer that pure rapture, which arises only from the
hearing of great music greatly played. Most
musicians need all this, as a challenge to their wits,
or as a daily spiritual food. To those the *prix de
Rome* must have come as an exceeding doubtful
privilege.

Nor should one make any mistake about the

prize itself. If it be a guarantee that a certain ability has been exhibited, it is certainly no more than that. The winning of it may seem to hold out rosy promises for the winner. As a matter of fact, the reality has often contrasted very tragically with the generous hopes and sanguine prophecies. One can easily deceive oneself. The simple truth of the matter is that men who won the laurel wreath and ultimately became famous, men like Halévy, Berlioz, Gounod, Bizet and Massenet, increased the prestige of the prize. Had Berlioz done nothing more than obtain the votes of the jury with his *Sardanapalus*, he would to-day be a name in a dictionary. On the other hand, men who won the laurel and eventually proved that their only distinction lay in a sad lack of that quality are to-day names in dictionaries, and not imposing ones even there. Who, I ask, knows anything of Rabuteau, the winner of 1868, to be found later playing the violin in the Théâtre Déjazet ? What does music owe to Blondeau, the victor of 1808, already named ? No person of critical acumen, I believe, will assert that Lenepveu, the favoured one of 1865, cut a very imposing figure. There is another side to the medal. Saint-Saëns competed twice for the prize, in 1852 and in 1864. In the former year the jury preferred Léonce Cohen ; in the latter Victor Sieg. His failure to gain the prize was one of the unique incidents in Saint-Saëns's career, a career so dazzlingly successful that he could almost afford a temporary set-back which threw into relief his triumphs and achievements. As for poor Sieg, he parried a kind of reproach to the end of his days. " When anyone speaks of me," Sieg is reported to have exclaimed, "he says, with a shrug of the shoulders, ' Sieg, a good musician ; it was he who ousted Saint-Saëns.'" But Saint-Saëns might have found consolation, if a man of his temper needed it, in the fact that others, who added to the glory of French music, never went to Rome as pensioners of the state. Auber, Félicien David, Lalo, Reyer, and Delibes managed to exist without the laurel wreath ; without the embraces of the officials, masters, parents, sisters, and cousins that were wont to follow the performance of the chosen work.

Full of high hopes, Bizet departed from Paris as the year 1857 ran to its close. He arrived in Rome on the 27th of January, 1858, exactly three days before the date on which the holder of the prize must present himself. In the interval, he had covered as much ground as would have satisfied the hustling tourist of that time. Along the route he chose were numberless scenes likely to impress themselves upon the mind of an observant and intelligent traveller. He went first to Lyons ; thereafter he visited in turn, Vienne, Valence, Orange, Avignon, Nîmes, Arles, Marseilles, Toulon, and Nice. Nice he left by diligence on the 2nd of January. Genoa was reached on the 5th. From Genoa he sailed to Leghorn, without

being seasick, as he dutifully reported to his
mother. Pisa, Pistoia, Lucca and Florence followed. In a few short weeks his eyes had been
opened. He had seen many famous places,
visited cathedrals, wandered in gardens filled with
exotic blooms, examined the masterpieces guarded
jealously in museums. Of his published letters
as a whole something will be said later. It is
enough to observe, in passing, that those addressed
to his people in Paris, which belong to this period,
are such as one would expect. The opening of
the letter which he wrote to his parents from
Avignon breathes the familiar accents of nos-
talgia. " The three days that I have passed far
away from you," he said, " have seemed to me
very long, and when I think that they are only the
three hundred and sixty-fifth part of the time I
have to be separated from you, I am dismayed."
He does not forget to recount incidents of the
journey, which are described in the manner of
most travellers, and he chatters very freely about his
comrades. Friends at home occupy his thoughts.
As soon as he closes his eyes at night, he dreams
of Paris. By the end of December (1857) he
has worn out two pairs of shoes—a piece of mis-
fortune attributed to the rocky heights he has
been climbing. Naturally, he is full of the different places visited. While the Corniche road won
his admiration, his entry into Italy did not. He
speaks of horrible architecture and pasteboard
churches. Over Florence he waxes enthusiastic.

What artists Raphael and Andrea del Sarto were ! The life and movement of the Tuscan city, far from escaping his notice, leads him to wonder why a country so glorious should have fallen into a condition so besotted.

A warm reception awaited Bizet and those who had travelled with him when the little group arrived at the Villa Medici, their abode. As the room he was to occupy had not yet been vacated, he found himself consigned to another, which, with its Turkish fittings, took his fancy. The food proved to be simple and excellent. And, if his heart beat fast with excitement at the novelty of all that lay around him, need one be surprised ? Fate did not smile so kindly upon every young fellow who sought fame and fortune along the dangerous paths of music.

After he had had time to look about him, Bizet chanted the grandeur that was Rome. By May he was all enthusiasm. " The more I see of Rome, the more I am enraptured," he wrote to his father. With his artist's eye, he watched the sunrise and the sunset. He longed to return in the future to write music in such a delectable spot. One could work better there than in Paris. Taking stock of himself and of his fortunes, and realising how much there was around him to minister to his needs, he found it difficult to understand those musicians who had regarded their sojourn at the Villa Medici as a grievous waste of time. The laureates who had achieved

23

something, Halévy, Thomas, Gounod, Berlioz, and Massé, spoke of Rome with deep emotion ; others blamed the years lost there for their sub-sequent failure. So he argued for Rome, forget-ting, in the intensity of his feelings, that the views of Berlioz hardly lent support to his case. He wandered in the Campagna, and discovered to his joy that the Appian way suited his mood. With boyish glee he participated in the Carnival, which took place shortly after his arrival, and, drinking his fill of the fun and frolic, appeared at a masked ball dressed as an infant, an appropriate choice for the future composer of *Jeux d'Enfants.* At this function he made a brave show in the beautiful costume put together for him by the wife of one of the servants at the Villa Medici. He did not lack social recreations. Soon, indeed, he struck up several friendships that added to the joy of life. With Count de Kisseleff, the Russian Ambassador, a man of taste, he must have had a great deal in common, for he dined at his Excel-lency's table frequently. One evening, he opened the eyes of a circle of friends by his exceeding skill at the piano, though he modestly hinted that his playing seemed wonderful because Italy had no pianists. In that fair land anyone who could strike a chord with two hands was a great artist, he humorously observed. Italy might be the land of song ; Bizet did not find it a land echoing great music. Bad taste, in his opinion, poisoned the country. It was lost to noble art. Rossini,

Mozart, Weber, Paër, Cimarosa were unknown, misunderstood, or forgotten.

The delights and advantages of travel are not lost upon those who have once packed their bags, bade good-bye to their habitual environment, and made their way to new scenes. Bizet had already seen a good deal of Northern Italy. He evidently looked forward to the moment when he would be able to take the road again. In May, 1859 an opportunity presented itself. For political reasons Venice and Naples, two places which he naturally longed to visit, were ruled out of the itinerary. Any disappointment he felt on this score was fully compensated for by the beauty of what he did see ; for the tour, though modest, proved entirely enjoyable. It was spent among the mountains and lasted for six weeks or so. " The trip I am making just now," he wrote to his mother from Anagni, " has never been undertaken by a musician." Shortly afterwards, on the 4th of August, he left Rome again, this time for Naples, to pass a few hours with Tiberius and Nero, as he put it in a letter to Marmontel. The Gulf of Naples impressed him more favourably than the town, or its inhabitants. Sorrento he described as the most beautiful paradise of the kingdom. The Latin authors assumed an immense interest for him as he walked amid the ruins of Pompeii. By the beginning of November, he was back in his old quarters, the richer in ideas, if not in pocket.

Before saying anything about the music which Bizet composed when in Rome, it is worth while to point out that the years of his exile were very exciting ones in a political sense. The figures of Victor Emmanuel, Cavour, Garibaldi and Pope Pius IX swept across the giant stage of European history. Early in 1859, the Austrians crossed the Ticino, and the French occupied Genoa. An insurrection in the Papal States took place in the following June. The Pope appealed to Europe against the King of Sardinia. Garibaldi called the Italians to arms. These, and many other momentous happenings, absorbed the attention of studious men, and excited the populace. Bizet did not find all the doors of Rome open to a young artist, however favoured by Nature. It is not difficult to account for the circumstance. In the first place, Roman society is one of the most exclusive in Europe. In the second, as can easily be understood if the tangled skein of history be unravelled, the French were not always loved very dearly in Italy during this disturbed period. The Italian museums, country-side and churches were open to the world ; the blue sky furnished a canopy for just and unjust, for Frenchmen and natives. The houses alone were closed against the foreigner. Bizet, I believe, held politicians in small esteem. If one asked him during those fateful years what he thought of the game, the moves and counter-moves, the appeals and passages of arms, he

would probably have replied that he had little taste
for such things.   He could not banish the thought
that a vast amount of the rhetoric and eloquence,
so beloved of public men, wrapt in high-sounding
phrases foolishness and futility.   On this or that
question he would surely enough have taken his
stand, or expressed his view ; and he could, on
occasion, deliver his opinion with unmistakable
emphasis.   But, unless I am grievously in error,
he regarded the politician's activities as transient
ones, the importance of which was vastly over-
rated by the law-abiding citizen, who digested his
newspaper religiously.   He was an artist.   He
had not only that which is called the artistic
temperament, but the artist's standard of values.
Those thus constituted will often find themselves
in disagreement with the prevailing view.   Bizet
saw the truth through an artist's eye.   He would
never have placed the man of affairs and the
creator of great and beautiful works upon the
same platform.

His life, during the years of his tenure of the
prix de Rome, did not lack the recreations and
relaxations so dear to the heart of Youth.   As I
have shown, he covered much ground ; he made
himself familiar with many of the scenes, monu-
ments, churches, and pictures that are double
starred in Baedeker ; he moved among the people ;
he passed hours in the company of friends with
whom he discovered some real point of contact ;
and, when he had a chance, as at the Carnival, he

27

engaged in those escapades that add to the joy of the student's existence. In addition to all this, he devoted time to a study of the Italian language, in which he, apparently, gained a measure of proficiency ; and he did some reading in the quiet hours left to him. It will be seen that in Italy he was not entirely idle. Whatever he may have been, he was not a musical Micawber. He did not wait for something to turn up. If he seldom failed to take advantage of the delights which the pensioner was at liberty to enjoy, he remembered the obligations of his office. He was a musician ; that fact he never forgot. To make his way in the world he knew that he had to work hard, to plough his own furrow. The good fairy who dictates immortal masterpieces and traces upon virgin-white music-paper scores worthy to be heard is a fiction dearly loved of shallow romanticism. She lives only in that superficial world. Bizet had no foolish illusions about this matter. He knew that if he took his place among the French musicians of his time it must be by dint of his own exertions, and by them alone.

The three obligatory works which he wrote during his exile were *Don Procopio*, an *opéra bouffe* in two acts, *Vasca da Gama*, a symphonic ode with chorus, and an orchestral suite made up of a scherzo and funeral march. That he should have addressed himself to those subjects is in itself not without significance. The first-named reflects his pre-occupa-

tion with Italian music at the period of its composition. The second seems to prove that he
desired to show what he could do in a dramatic
way. The third intimates that Bizet, though he
was strongly attracted by the theatre, did not
overlook the possibilities of symphonic music.
He had, indeed, an ambition to shine as a symphonic writer. To the symphonies already in
existence he wished to add one that should carry
his name, one that should prove to concert-goers
his ability to express himself in purely intrumental
terms. While the fact does not seem to be an
unusual one, it must be remarked that the theatre
has played a predominant part in French music.
Its lure was all but irresistible. At the time of
which I speak, a composer making a bid for
recognition had to knock very persistently at the
doors of the theatre. That Bizet, though primarily occupied with opera, took a larger view is
plain. He must be allowed credit for having
taken that view when it was not so common in
France as it is to-day. He loved the stage, no
doubt, but he was not insensible to the chaster
beauties of the symphonic muse.

Don Procopio owes its existence to one of those
freaks of fate which, insignificant in themselves,
mould events in the lives of men. Wandering
about Rome, Bizet one day picked up a volume at
the stall of a second-hand bookseller. Dipping
into it, he found in its pages the making of an
Italian farce in the *genre* of *Don Pasquale*. As he

had for some time vainly sought a subject that appealed to him, one is not far wrong in assuming that his discovery was extremely welcome, in that it promised the profitable employment of his pen. He attacked the composition of the *opéra bouffe* with zest. The writing of it gave him the keenest of pleasure. He was much amused at some of the situations, and so sure of success that he anticipated a favourable verdict from the Académie des Beaux-Arts in Paris, the body charged with the duty of reporting on the works sent from Rome, though he had substituted an opera of the lightest character for a mass, as the rules demanded.

The report, in so far as it dealt with the music, was of an encouraging nature. After mentioning in a general way the progress shown by the young artist, it touched on those passages by which the judges had been arrested : here a piquant effect, there a melody delicately accompanied, and so forth. The composer, it chronicled, exhibited a marked bent for the lighter style. No young musician could have asked much more. Bizet looked upon this official communication as a spur to further effect. It raised his spirits, made him more confident than ever, and nourished his hopes for the future. But the academic voices of Paris had not yet subsided into silence. There were, as it happened, two reports on such works. The second, of a more confidential nature than the first, was not printed, but sent direct to the composer concerned, and it contained some well-meant advice. In this second report the ruling powers took Bizet to task for having written an *opéra bouffe* when the regulations stipulated for a mass. They reminded him that the most sprightly natures found in the contemplation of sublime subjects a style indispensable even for light productions, a style without which a work cannot last. This report bore the signature of Ambroise Thomas.

But the finding, the writing, and the judging of this little piece did not exhaust its curious history. The works sent from Rome, it seems, having been duly examined, were, at this period, consigned to a sort of lumber-room. There they reposed in glorious confusion. Whether the pontifical pronouncements were glowing, or damning, it mattered not. The authorities evidently felt assured that, their fiery ordeal past, the scores could not possibly retain any modicum of interest for posterity—hardly a compliment to young France. For some years *Don Procopio* could not be traced. It appeared to be irretrievably lost, and Pigot shed a tear over its disappearance. In 1895, when all save one or two historians must, surely, have dismissed it from their thoughts—if it ever occupied them—it turned up among some documents that had belonged to Auber. In 1906, nearly half a century after its composition, it occupied the stage for the first time, and the stage which it did occupy was that of Monte Carlo. Remembering its origin, the verdict

passed upon it, its long sleep amid the dust and
cobwebs, and its subsequent recovery, one arrives
at the conclusion that the theatre, which, above all
others, had a claim upon it was the one standing
within a stone's throw of the famous Casino.

In the summer of 1860 Bizet left Rome. He
proposed to visit a few of the Italian cities which
he did not know. To this end he mapped out a
tour that embraced Ravenna, Venice, Verona,
Padua and Milan. Paris he would enter at the
beginning of December. But " the best-laid
schemes of mice and men gang aft agley". In
September he reached Venice, where distressing
news awaited him. His mother was seriously
ill. For a considerable time her health had been
a matter of deep concern. In October, 1858, he
wrote her a letter in which there are traces, more
than faint, of some anxiety. He was disquieted
by the receipt of news regarding her state of health
in March of the following year. Yet, apprehensive as he must have been for many months, the
crisis, when it came, darkened his spirit and threw
a gloom over all things. Fortunately, he had
with him Guiraud, a close friend who shared his
joys and sorrows ; Guiraud who could, at least,
offer the poor consolation one can give at such
moments. Bizet tells how in his frenzy he would
have strangled a gondolier had not his boon
companion intervened.[1] When great issues are

[1] Letter of 5th September 1860. See *Lettres de Georges Bizet*,
Preface de Louis Ganderax.

at stake and danger threatens, men see things in a
way they never saw them before. What appeared to them valuable loses its value ; what they
took for granted becomes the most cherished
desire of their hearts. Compared with this
desire all else is small and futile and meaningless.
The strange change, to which we are all subject,
manifests itself in the letter just referred to.
Bizet had been working to build up a reputation ;
he had met with successes, which gave birth to
sanguine expectations. Of a sudden, these things
appeared as nought. His victories and his hopes,
his toil and his fame—what were they to him at
this tragic hour ? He may have heard, wafted
across the lagoons, the voices of the gondoliers
intoning the " Solemn Tune " to which the
stanzas of Tasso were set—a tune that by
reason of its grave beauty had left its mark
upon Addison and Liszt ; if he did, the
melancholy music must have ministered to his
mood. For in Venice the composer was lost in
the son.

He hurried on to Paris, anxiety gnawing at his
heart. On his arrival his mother rallied somewhat, only to suffer a relapse. In a few days
the end came peacefully ; it was well he had
not tarried by the way. Just when the sun
shone most benignly, when the future greeted
him with outstretched arms, a blow most cruel
fell upon him—a blow which gives the note
of pathos to a simple sentence he had written

almost three years before, "What joy on my
return !"[1]

He could not afford to rest upon his oars. He
was youthful and active. He believed in his star.
To the tranquil scenes his eyes had rested upon
during these last three years he could not have
found a greater contrast than the bustling streets
of Paris. The movement and life of Paris, to
which he had been for so long a stranger, must
have stirred a man of his nature very deeply.
There were influential people whose interest he
might be lucky enough to engage. There were
doors which he might be lucky enough to find
open to him. But was he known beyond the
circle of his friends and admirers ? The doubt
may have crossed his mind. Three years' absence
is a long one, and the memory of a public immersed
in the affairs of the day is short. In one of the
essays which appear in his *Harmonie et Mélodie*,
Saint-Saëns writes that the musician returned from
Rome is a legendary figure ; that his sojourn in
the Eternal City only served to make him forgotten, supposing that he were ever known. It,
therefore, remained for Bizet to furnish incontestable proof that he was a man to be reckoned
with, and not one of those mediocrities, who, by
a whimsical turn of fate, had grasped the *prix de
Rome*. The Chinese, who are a wise people, have
a saying which runs : " If you have a loaf, sell half
of it and buy a lily". This is a beautiful saying,

[1] Letter of 29th December, 1857.

worthy of all acceptation. In these few words one has as concise a reproof to materialism as one could desire. Man does not live by bread alone, but as man, in a very real sense, does live by bread, there remains something more to be said. The problem which so often confronts the young artist is not the parting with a half-loaf for a lily ; it is the acquiring of so much as a modest fragment of that simple article of diet. Dreams do not bring much at the fair, and aspirations, however noble, are unquoted on the bourse.

Bizet took the only course a sensible man could conceivably have taken. He plunged into work, and, realising that one has to eat humble-pie before one can sip the nectar of the gods, he did not disdain the task which came his way. At this period he arranged for the pianoforte a large number of popular pieces selected from French, German and Italian sources. In their entirety these transcriptions were published in 1865, under the name of *Le Pianiste Chanteur*. While no one will be tempted to call this a very inspiring occupation, the result was, at least, calculated to bring his name before a large circle of pianists, and, considering his own enormous pianistic ability, the task cannot have been so irksome as was the soulless hackwork undertaken by Wagner in Paris some twenty years previously.

But Bizet was not entirely occupied by these transcriptions. He worked at the score of an opera entitled *La Guzla de l'Emir*, the book of which was by Michel Carré and Jules Barbier. He must have finished the score, because we read that it was in rehearsal at the Opéra Comique. About this time, however, Carvalho, manager of the Théatre Lyrique, approached him in connection with another work. Count Walewski, a man of fine taste and wide culture, had bestowed a sub-vention of 100,000 francs on this theatre, the object of his generosity being to help young musicians, who seemed to him to be at a dis-advantage compared with the masters who had made their names. A condition of his gift was that each year the theatre should produce a work in three acts composed by one of those young men. Carvalho was deeply impressed by the personality and intelligence of Bizet, so impressed, indeed, that he handed him the libretto of an opera in three acts by Michel Carré and Cormon, entitled *Les Pêcheurs de Perles*. Bizet withdrew the work on which he had just been engaged and com-menced upon the new subject, which seems to have taken his fancy. The score of *La Guzla de l'Emir* must have been destroyed by its author himself, as no trace of it is to be discovered. The book was used by another French musician, namely, Theodore Dubois, whose version was produced in 1873.

The first representation of *Les Pêcheurs de Perles* took place on the 29th of September, 1863, and the work attained eighteen performances. Its reception seems to have been rather curious.

The production had been evidently keenly anticipated by many of those who knew, or had heard
of, Bizet. On the historic evening the public,
so far as one can learn, was more curious about
the music and surprised at the hearing of it than
pleased with it. At the termination of the opera,
a circle of friends enthusiastically hailed the composer, who must have been encouraged by this
manifestation of goodwill. Among those on whom
Les Pêcheurs de Perles made a favourable impression
was Berlioz, and he recorded his verdict in *Les
Débats*. " The score of this opera," he said, " has
attained a real success. It contains a considerable number of beautiful and expressive pieces,
full of fire and of a rich colour." His criticism
finished with the remark that the opera redounded
to the credit of Bizet and that one would be forced
to accept him as a composer, in spite of his rare
talent as a pianist. The rest of the press was
hardly so encouraging.

The man was not insensitive to criticism, but,
according to Edmond Galabert, who was on
intimate terms with him, he laboured under no
misconception regarding the worth of his music.
Galabert says that he did not know whether Bizet
was very much affected by the press criticisms of
Les Pêcheurs de Perles. One day, however, Galabert told the composer that he had bought the
score, at which piece of news Bizet in his annoyance, cried out : " What have you done that for ?
I would have given you mine. Besides, you will

have no need of it." After reading these words,
we are not astonished to learn that Bizet spoke of
this early production as a work which, apart from
one or two numbers, was without value.

Of Bizet's method of composition I shall have
something to say in the proper place, but I
must draw the reader's attention to the fact that
he was, at one time or another, enamoured of
many subjects. Those who know only his most
popular works would be surprised if they learned
how often he weighed the possibilities of a plot
merely to discard it. As has been related, he
finished *La Guzla de l'Emir*, withdrew it, and
ultimately destroyed it. In some cases, his fancy
played about a theme, but the serious task of
composition was never entered upon. In others,
he made considerable headway with the music,
but never put a note of it on paper. All this, I
think, argues a mental alertness ; it might even
be said that it argues a yielding to impulse. A
book or dramatic situation was brought to his
attention when his imagination was on the wing.
As in a flash, he saw what he conceived to be its
musical value ; he would furnish it with the
setting, which could not fail to add to its appeal.
If some of those projected operas were never
begun, one can but surmise that the impulse did
not last long. If some absorbed his energies to
be renounced later, one can only hazard the guess
that he revised his verdict of them in the calmer
moments of reflection. If others which took

shape in his mind never reached the manuscript paper, one naturally assumes that a theme either better suited to his gift or of an attraction more potent and enduring stood in the way of their production.

Les Pêcheurs de Perles was an accomplished fact. It had been written, produced, and criticised. Whatever he thought of the work and its reception, Bizet's path was mapped out alike by his ambition and peculiar powers. What could a composer do but compose? How could he hope to reach the heights save by an assiduous cultivation of his talents? Forthwith he gave himself up to a five-act opera, called *Ivan le Terrible*. He completed the score and offered it to the manager of the Théâtre Lyrique, who accepted it. Then a strange thing happened ; he withdrew his work. The rest of the story is soon told. At some later date, it is believed, he consigned his manuscript to the flames.

In view of the facts, one cannot expect to acquire much knowledge of this piece at the hands of those who have written about Bizet's compositions. Pigot, who devotes more space to it than others, expresses a view which may account for what seems a singular proceeding on the part of a youthful composer eager to grasp " the skirts of happy chance." According to him, after Bizet had completed *Les Pêcheurs de Perles*, he fell under the influence of Verdi. *Ivan le Terrible* reflected this influence. The biographer calls to mind that all through his life Bizet professed a great admiration for Verdi, but, he adds, this lasting admiration had nothing in common with the passing infatuation from which he was then suffering. Pigot did not believe that Bizet wrote this score unconsciously in the Verdian manner. The composer's intelligence would have prevented anything in the nature of a foolish surrender. What he did believe was that Bizet, searching for the right mode of expression, thought that he had found it in a union of two styles ; the one Verdian and the other French. No other explanation of Bizet's action has, so far as I know, been advanced. Be the reason what it may, the action in itself appears to me to indicate no little courage, I might almost say conscience, in a man of his years and circumstances. Rising composers, similarly placed, might be pardoned if they sighed a sigh of relief when a theatrical manager looked favourably upon their five-act works. Galabert mentions that Bizet did not tell him about *Ivan le Terrible*.[1] The silence of the composer leads one to think that he held the music in no very high esteem.

Something that evidently met with more approval as it took shape in his hands soon kept him as fully occupied as ever. Carvalho entrusted him with the libretto of an opera in four acts by De Saint-Georges and Adenis. *Les Pêcheurs de*

[1] Georges Bizet : *Lettres à un Ami*, Introduction de Edmund Galabert.

Perles plays itself out in the sunny and luxurious island of Ceylon.   He now found himself carried off, as on the magic carpet of the East, to latitudes far less sunny, far less luxurious.   The book which lay before him awaiting its musical accompaniment bore the title, *La Jolie Fille de Perth*, and was an adaptation of Sir Walter Scott's novel. He completed the score speedily.   Writing in July, 1866, he told Galabert that he had signed the contract.   By September he was able to inform his friend that the first act had been finished.   In a third letter, of January, 1867, he intimated the delivery of the entire score to Carvalho.   If these dates tell their own tale of hard work and concentration, they do not tell everything.   With a reluctance which can be readily understood, he performed other, less heroic, duties.   Six songs, which belong to this active time, were dashed off *au galop*.   Solos for the cornet took up two valuable days.   Little wonder is it that he exclaimed : " I work enormously." [1]

While turned out so expeditiously, the opera did not go into rehearsal at once ; far from it. Various circumstances accounted for the delay. London, for example, claimed Nilsson, for whom the rôle of Catherine was written.   The months dragged on wearily, and by the time *La Jolie Fille de Perth* occupied the boards of the Théatre Lyrique a year had run its course.   On the 26th of December, 1867, the opera made its début.

[1] Letter to Galabert, September 1866.

D

The press gave the composer little grounds for
dissatisfaction. His opera had, in his own phrase,
obtained a true success.[1] He had not looked for
a reception so enthusiastic and, at the same time,
so critical. He had been kept in suspense, had
been taken seriously, and had known the pleasure
of moving and thrilling a house, not exactly
friendly. Apparently the favour thus bestowed
was to seek at later performances. The great
public, or that part of it which made acquaintance
with the opera subsequently, remained cold.
After twenty-one performances, *La Jolie Fille de
Perth* was withdrawn. In the Spring of the
following year it was heard at Brussels. According
to Bizet himself the rendering was " monstrous."[2]
This notwithstanding, the opera satisfied the
musical public of the Belgian capital, and had a
good press.

A few days before the first performance of *La
Jolie Fille de Perth* there was introduced to the
patrons of the Théatre de l'Athénée an operetta in
four acts, *Malbrough s'en va t'en guerre.* Though
the piece pleased immensely, it would probably
have been soon forgotten but for its composite
authorship. Four musicians, Bizet, Legouix,
Emile Jonas, and Delibes had a hand in the music.
Each contributed an act, Bizet's share consisting
of the first. There is no evidence that he attached

[1] Letter to Galabert, January 1868.

[2] Hugues Imbert : *Portraits et Etudes.* Tenth letter to Paul
Lacombe.

any importance to this incursion into the lighter domain. Indeed, he spoke of his having " knocked off" (*baclé*) the portion allotted to him.[1]

It will be gathered that he had for some little time been working at pretty high pressure in an effort to establish a reputation and satisfy his daily needs. He was to have little respite. Just as *La Jolie Fille de Perth* captured the stage, a competition in which it might be worth his while to participate was announced. Intending composers were to try their skill on a piece that would be mounted at the Opéra. Early in the following year the subject, *La Coupe du Roi de Thulé*, the poem by Louis Gallet and Edouard Blau, had been chosen. After some deliberation and encouragement, Bizet began to work at it. By October, 1868, he had finished the first two acts, with which he was delighted.[2] Then, for all his satisfaction, he changed his mind. From a fresh quarter, the Opéra Comique, came a demand for a new work. This seemed fruitful of results. On the type of opera indicated he nursed ideas he would be glad to put into practice. For this, and for other reasons, he shelved *La Coupe du Roi de Thulé*.

Before he could record a semiquaver of the *opéra-comique* which he was so anxious to write, other duties invited his attention. Halévy, his old teacher, had died in 1862, leaving unfinished

---

[1] Sixth letter to Lacombe.
[2] Letter to Galabert, October 1868.

Noë, a three-act biblical opera on a libretto by De Saint-Georges. What had yet to be done to *Noë* asked for disinterestedness, patience, and ability. Than the completing of an opera left in skeleton form I can conceive of few more thankless tasks. If the result be success, the credit will go, in large measure, to the dead ; if it be failure, the public is likely to fasten on the living scapegoat. The finishing process is always unsatisfactory. The audience is mystified as to what portion belongs to one partner, and what to the other. The partnership itself is unfair. For the nonce, it exposes the reputation of the dead to the caprice of the living ; and it presumes in the latter not only an uncanny knowledge of the ways and means commonly employed by the former, but, in the endeavour to obtain a uniformity of style, imposes a repression of self abominable to musicians of strong character. It is, so far as the finishing composer is concerned, a " heads you win, tails I lose " proposition.

The relations which existed between Halévy and his protégé were so cordial that Bizet seemed to be the man best fitted to take up *Noë*. If anyone had the necessary qualifications, it was the brilliant pupil and close friend of the departed musician. Not only had Bizet studied with Halévy ; he understood Halévy's nature. From his intercourse with the older master, he had gained an insight into his character and the workings of his mind.

44

He undertook the hazardous business not, I
imagine, without trepidation. Bravely, he grasped
the threads, deliberated as to what he should do,
and endeavoured to make progress. Problems
and obstacles soon presented themselves in plenty ;
he could not get into his stride. Dissatisfied, he
put *Noë* aside. This happened in 1868. But
the following year was to witness a second trial
with the same book. In the interval, an event of
great importance to him took place. On the
9th of June, 1869, he married Mlle. Geneviève
Halévy, daughter of his master. Perhaps, in
passing, one who has the privilege of her friendship may be permitted to speak of this lady's
loyalty to Bizet's memory, which is matched only
by her unfailing kindness.

Shortly after, Bizet returned to the biblical
work, this time completing it. In a letter of
October, 1869, he reported progress.[1] Two acts
had been delivered ; the third was due by the
25th of October, the fourth[2] by the 15th of
November. He reserved to himself the right to
make decisions affecting the cast. The bass and
the first soprano were wanting. If he could not
find them, *Noë* would have to wait. Little did he
think, when he penned these words, how many
troubles lay ahead of him. The Théatre Lyrique,
for which *Noë* was destined, became bankrupt.
Then there happened something which shook
Europe to its depths, affecting more things than

---

[1] To Galabert. [2] This presumably refers to sc. 11 of Act 111.

the fate of posthumous operas—the Franco-Prussian War. One almost feels that *Noë* was a misnomer ; a piece with such a history should have been called *Job*. Not till 1885 did it make a public appearance, and this took place not on French soil, but at the Grand Ducal Theatre of Carlsruhe under Felix Mottl. According to a despatch in *Le Figaro*, the performance lacked nothing in splendour. This initial blaze of glory has had no successor. France has yet to hear *Noë*.

It has already been observed that Bizet wished to add lustre to his name by the composition of a symphony. As early as 1860 he had written from Rimini to his mother informing her that he had a notion to write a symphony to be entitled, *Rome, Venice, Florence and Naples.*[1] Rome would provide the first movement, Venice the andante, Florence the scherzo, and Naples the finale. It was a new idea, he believed. While this early scheme never matured, he did contribute something to the concert repertory. It occupied him off and on for about two years. He played over themes for the first movement to Galabert in May, or June, 1866. To the same friend he wrote in June, 1868, that he had finished his symphony. In October he owned his dissatisfaction with the finale. By the following March he was able to speak of the reception given to the work :

[1] *Cf.* Richard Strauss's *Aus Italien.*

" My symphony has gone very well. First movement—
a round of applause, followed by demands for silence, second
round of applause, one hiss, third round of applause ; andante
—a round of applause ; finale—great effect, three rounds of
applause, silence, two or three hisses. Altogether success. " [1]

The history of the piece is, like the history of
much of Bizet's music, more than a little curious.
As a testimony of his progress, he had sent from
Rome to Paris, among other things, a scherzo.
This scherzo appeared on one of the programmes
of the Concerts Pasdeloup on the 11th of January
1863, without gaining the success that awaited it
when it was repeated shortly afterwards under
the auspices of the Société Nationale des Beaux-
Arts. The scherzo, however, was but a fragment,
and as such did not satisfy Bizet's longings. He
thought of Beethoven and Mendelssohn, whose
symphonic compositions encouraged him to emu-
lation. In 1866 he tackled his new score in real
earnest. The result was heard under Pasdeloup
on the 28th of February, 1869. It then went by
the name of *Souvenirs de Rome*, was described as a
fantaisie symphonique, and had three movements
called, respectively, *Une chasse dans la forêt d'Ostie*,
Une Procession, and *Carnaval à Rome*. After one
performance, the symphony slept undisturbed
for eleven years. Not until 1880 did it again
invade the concert hall. When it did, the name
had been altered to *Roma*, and the scherzo was
restored. In its final form the work consists of

[1] Letter to Galabert, March 1869.

47

four numbers—-an introduction and allegro, andante, scherzo, and carnaval. It was published
thus in 1880.

We have now arrived at that tragic year 1870,
when the raucous voice of war, arch-enemy of
culture, drowned that of music. The outbreak of
hostilities played woeful havoc with artistic affairs
and upset the plans of peace-loving, sedentary
musicians. Saint-Saëns joined the National
Guard. In the ranks of a *bataillon de marche*
Massenet contrived to cultivate his talent, while
Prussian guns punctuated the fragments which
he wrote. Like his two confrères, Bizet lived
through strange days. He became a fusilier in
the 6th Battalion of the National Guard. Looking below the surface of things, he saw that all
was not well. He did not share the easy optimism
of those who scented the approach of glorious
victory. A valuable glimpse of his state of mind
is to be had in a brief letter, which he wrote in
August, 1870 :

> " And our poor philosophy, our dreams of universal peace,
> of cosmopolitan fraternity, of human association ! . . . In
> place of these, tears, blood, devastation, crimes without
> number and without end. I am not able to tell you, my dear
> friend, into what sadness these hours plunge me. I remember
> that I am French, but I am not able to forget that I am a man.
> This war will cost humanity five hundred thousand lives.
> As for France, she will lose all." [1]

Well might he ponder. The impending catastrophe, which involved the downfall of the second

[1] To Galabert.

Empire, meant national humiliation and un-
paralleled loss of military prestige. It meant also
the end of the Paris he had known ; the Paris
which had danced and capered so joyfully in the
assurance that France was " ready to the last
button " ; the Paris whose taste had been so
accurately gauged by the adept and wily Offenbach ; the Paris which sat so adoringly at the feet
of Hortense Schneider, " la grande duchesse de
Gerolstein." A later generation has learnt most
tragically how deep and widespread is the effect
of war upon the gentler arts of peace. Bizet, his
head full of schemes, cannot have been blind to
the changes that were being wrought before his
very eyes.

But not for long were his thoughts seriously
diverted from future production. In March,
1871, he wrote to Paul Lacombe that he wished
to have his two operas ready for the autumn. The
reference is, presumably, to *Grisélidis* and *Clarissa
Harlowe*. Of them I shall have something to say
when dealing with the pieces which he never
brought to fruition. " If the theatres are open,"
he continued, " I shall manage to hold my own,
but if not, I do not know to what kind of work I
shall turn in order to make a living." [1] A month
later he opened his heart to Mme. Halévy :

> " This will be no place for honest folk. . . . I shall have to
> emigrate. Shall I go to Italy, England or America ? . . .
> Altogether I am completely discouraged and have nothing to

[1] Eleventh letter to Lacombe.

hope for here. Germany, the country of music, is impossible for all who have a French name and heart." [1]

As for the result of the war on his music, that is to be looked for in the dramatic overture *Patrie*, first performed under the redoubtable Pasdeloup on the 15th of February, 1874. In composing it, he obviously wished to give voice to the sufferings of the nation, but in the writing his thoughts turned to Poland, a country of unhappy memories. The whole may, therefore, be called a picture of national distress, which gives place to one of joy and victory. The most striking passage is that in which the violoncelli announce a funeral march to accompaniment of brass. To this succeeds a note of confidence in the major ; a Lisztian antithesis. The *lamento* is swallowed up in the final *trionfo*.

In his next stage work he returned to the East. Ceylon provided the background for *Les Pêcheurs de Perles*, Egypt that for *Djamileh*, a one-act *opéra-comique*, the words of which are by Louis Gallet.[2] Brought out at the Opéra Comique on the 22nd of March, 1872, this little piece marked Bizet's renewed contact with the stage. Almost five years had passed since he sought the approval of the opera-goer with *La Jolie Fille de Perth*. In view of the length of this interval, in view of the world-shaking events which had transpired during

[1] Ganderax.
[2] The libretto was at first called *Namouna*, and is thus referred to by Bizet in a letter of January 1872 to Galabert, and in the eighteenth letter to Lacombe.

it, in view of what he had already done, and in view of his age, the curiosity of those anxious to keep abreast of the times should have been keen, if it were not. But there was a post-war public to reckon with ; a post-war public no doubt rendered restless by the unexampled experiences through which it had but lately passed. It might, perhaps, have been pardoned a certain aloofness at the *première*, especially as the work itself is distinguished rather for charm and delicacy than for strength and dramatic intensity. Taking into account the date of its production and the conditions in which that production was made, the reception at first offered to *Djamileh* may be put down as remarkably appreciative. The press was more than cordial. The first-night audience gave every encouragement. In his usual lively way Bizet kept his friends informed of what had occurred. Shortly after the début, he wrote to Paul Lacombe :

"*Djamileh* is not a success in the ordinary sense of the word. Mme. Prelly has been below mediocrity, and the piece is too far removed from the conventions of the Opéra Comique. For all that, the receipts are fair and the public listens with evident interest. The press has been excellent. The principal papers have praised the score, and the *Lundistes Melodistes*, while blaming my Wagnerian (?) tendencies, have treated me so seriously and so cordially that I am not worried by their criticisms. Whatever happens, I am content to return to the path that I should never have left, and that I shall never forsake again." [1]

[1] Fifteenth Letter to Lacombe.

In a letter to Galabert, penned in the following month, he repeated his conviction that *Djamileh* was not a success. He characterised the poem as anti-theatrical, but owned to being satisfied with the result. Never had an *opéra-comique* in one act been more seriously, more passionately, discussed. From the conviction that he had at last found his true path he derived more satisfaction than from the opinions of the critics.[1] But, as with *La Jolie Fille de Perth*, the first impression proved to be misleading. So quickly did the interest exhibited on the opening night diminish that *Djamileh* was withdrawn after only ten performances. In an oft-quoted sonnet, Saint-Saëns rapped the public of the day over the knuckles. *Djamileh* would pursue her golden dreams amid the roses, for ever disdaining the stupid throng.

While *Djamileh* passed quickly out of notice, Bizet's name did not long remain absent from the theatre bills. With his one-act *opéra-comique* he gave a good account of himself. In this line of work he found his true vocation, according to his own declaration. " It is at the Opéra Comique that I shine," he told Guiraud,[2] but he was about to bring forward additional proof of his musicianship in an entirely different sphere. Scarcely had *Djamileh* quitted the boards than Alphonse Daudet's *L'Arlésienne* occupied those of the Vaudeville. For this three-act piece Bizet wrote

[1] Letter to Galabert, 17th June 1872.
[2] Quoted by Pigot.

52

a score consisting of twenty-seven numbers. As *L'Arlésienne* was first heard on the 1st of October, 1872, it would seem that he did not linger long over what is generally regarded as one of his best efforts. The numbers, it is true, are not of great length ; some of them are, indeed, the merest fragments. Yet, after examining the quality of them, one is likely to come to the conclusion that his muse served him well. The term " incidental music," with its hint of the casual, is loosely employed. If the music associated with a play underlines the dramatic action, lends it character and atmosphere, or throws a mantle of poetry over the situations, it ought to be regarded as an integral part of the production. If it does not achieve this, if it stands apart from the drama, it is worse than useless. But, his score finished, the vexations of the composer are not likely to cease. The writer of what is called incidental music must be a born optimist. In the first place, he has to make allowance for the fact that he is not certain to have at his disposal either the musical resources or the technical accomplishment to be found in an opera house. In the second, he has to make allowance for the fact that some members of the audience will not trouble about his contribution to the general effect. There seems to be only one way out of this latter difficulty—to provide music of so virile a kind that even the least musical will be unable to overlook it, or employ it as a background for conversation. *L'Arlésienne* is the work of a practical man who kept in mind the means available to him. In spite of its merits (perhaps because of them—the public which first heard *L'Arlésienne* was a post-war public), in spite of its modest dimensions and direct appeal, it appears to have made little impression at the Vaudeville. Justice, if somewhat tardy, came shortly after, when the most important parts of the music were transferred to the concert room. In November of the same year, a selection of it had an honoured position in the programme of the Concerts Populaires de Cirque d'Hiver. "*L'Arlésienne* has been played on Sunday by Pasdeloup. Encore and great effect", wrote Bizet. From that date, it has gone on its way rejoicing, and now takes a proud place in the orchestral repertoire. There exist two suites : one by Bizet himself, one by his friend, Guiraud. More recently, Sir Landon Ronald, the editor of *Masters of Music*, has arranged a portion of the music for concert purposes, and this has won great favour with the audiences that have heard it.

Bizet could hardly complain that his works did not get a hearing. All things considered, his post-war achievements were not barren of result. He may not have caused the musical world of France to rock upon its foundations. He had, at least, produced a little opera which provoked discussion, and penned music that drew forth applause in concert. With the new year he addressed himself once more to the concertgoer—on this occasion with a *Petite Suite d'Or-chestre*. A little time previously, he had written twelve pieces for piano duet, called *Jeux d'Enfants*. The orchestral suite, comprising five of them, was heard at the Odéon under Edouard Colonne on the 2nd of March 1873, when it met with approval. It is interesting to observe that *Jeux d'Enfants* attracted the attention of Sigfrid Karg-Elert, who had the idea of scoring five numbers. He thought it worth while to give them an orchestral dress, sonorous, rich and full of colour, somewhat after the style of Mahler and Strauss.

" I know what I can do," said Bizet in a letter written just after the production of *Djamileh*. There can be no doubt that the man was gaining in confidence, in mastery, in knowledge of himself. All artistic endeavour is one long search for authentic self-expression. The artist has to prove all things, to sift the dross from the pure metal—a long and exhaustive process. He has to find his own voice if he is not to remain a feeble echo of other voices. Bizet must have derived some satisfaction from his recent labours. *Djamileh* could hardly be called an enormous financial success ; the music of *L'Arlésienne* did not strike dumb with admiration those who witnessed the play. But to one conscious of his own powers there remains compensation in that very consciousness, a real compensation to those of high aims. This firm belief in himself urges a man to fresh flights. The strong man increases his

strength by his exploits in the ring ; the swift
holds his own by matching himself against the
fleet of foot ; and the artist, likewise, returns to the
fray to gain the laurels of the victor. Bizet had
driven his pen industriously. Nothing was more
foreign to his thoughts than to lay it down. One
project after another passed through his mind.
A new theme immediately took the place vacated
by its predecessor. A score finished, he itched
to embark on fresh adventures, and he was about
to embark on the greatest adventure of his artistic
life. In June 1872, in a letter to Galabert, he let
fall a.hint concerning his next work :

> " I am asked to write three acts for the Opéra Comique—
> Meilhac and Halévy will do the piece. It will be bright
> (*gai*), but of a brightness that allows style."

The opera in question was *Carmen*. An
undated communication to Lacombe recorded
progress :

> " I have finished the first act of *Carmen*; I am quite content
> with it."

And later, to the same correspondent, he related
that he had taken two months to orchestrate the
twelve hundred pages of the score. *Carmen*,
however, occupies a position so important among
modern operas that the story of its production
must have a chapter to itself.

CHAPTER II

Production of *Carmen*—Not a Fiasco—First-night Audience—
Performance—Prudish Objections—Bizet and the Public—
Carmen and the Paris Press—Ludovic Halévy's Story—Old
" Père Dupin "—Galli-Marié's Testimony—Dislike of the
Tragic Termination—The Views of Some Musicians—Maurice
Lefèvre—Problem of Public Taste—Some Conclusions—Sub-
sequent Fortunes of the Opera—Its many Exponents—About
the Habanera.

Carmen, an *opéra-comique* in four acts, based
upon the story of the same name by Prosper
Mérimée, was produced at the Opéra Comique,
Paris, on the 3rd of March 1875, a date of the
first importance both in the life of Bizet and in the
history of French music.   There is still, I think,
a wide-spread belief that this charming work made
a complete fiasco, and that the passive indifference,
if not active hostility, of the public filled Bizet
with such hopeless despair that it hastened his
end.   The belief is strengthened by the senti-
mental romanticist who dwells in most of us.   We
get a perverse satisfaction from the thought that
the artist is poor, neglected, and misunderstood.
What the world calls success is associated with
Philistinism.   It is to be won by the savages of
civilisation, who know nothing of, and care little
for, the arts.   We see in the artist a figure far

removed from Croesus. We allot him an attic, dress him in the shabbiest of clothes, deny him a good meal, and, having formed this mental picture, feel that we have done him the completest justice. We are suspicious of success, because success is so often incapable of romance. To the popular imagination the artist will always be misunderstood, friendless, and poverty-stricken ; he will never be more than the emaciated hero, who wanders aimlessly through the vapid pages of a penny novelette. The danger of this assumption lies in the fact that it may very easily lead us to apply an erroneous 'test. Many artists have suffered cruelly ; but this is not to say that all artists have suffered cruelly, nor is it to say that the intensity of their sufferings is in proportion to their artistry. One must, therefore, guard against the foolish method of judging the artist according to his sufferings or failures. There are successes of which a man may reasonably be proud, and successes of which he ought to be ashamed. There are failures which are more successful than success itself, and failures lacking the touch of heroism.

At the risk of dissipating a romance, it behoves one to examine the available evidence, and speak of the reception of *Carmen* and its influence on Bizet as they are revealed in the light of the same. One need not dread the consequences. After all, Bizet wrote *Carmen*, which in itself is no small title to fame, and one ought to be fortified by the thought that the truth as one sees it is the best tribute one can offer to the artist. The sublime irony arises when a man's celebrity is based on apocryphal acts and romantic legends. If a man has the root of the matter in him, he need not fear the activities of those who frown upon tales, the authenticity of which is, to say the least, doubtful.

First, let me point out that *Carmen* did not collapse ignominiously after the historic first night. So far from this being the case, the opera attained the not disreputable total of thirty-seven performances. It is not, I admit, an astounding record ; it has been eclipsed by *The Merry Widow* and *Chu Chin Chow*. But if Bizet struck a new note and presented a score containing something that was then unusual and bizarre to a public rooted in tradition and of markedly conservative leanings, the record assumes a deeper significance. While the ways of impresarios are often strange, one can hardly believe that *Carmen* would have been permitted to remain so long upon the stage merely out of charity. The Opéra Comique is not, and never has been, so far as I am aware, a philanthropic institution.

Even more arresting is the action attributed to Camille du Locle, the director. On the 10th of March, exactly one week after the introduction of *Carmen*, *Le Figaro*, as Gauthier-Villars recounts, intimated that du Locle had approached Bizet with a proposal that he should write another opera on a book by Meilhac and Halévy, the librettists he had just served.[1] This, indeed, makes strange reading. Why should a theatrical director, at whose theatre an opera had missed fire, turn so quickly to the author of the failure in order to obtain a new work from him ? More than this ; the management of the Imperial Opera in Vienna was soon to negotiate for the production of *Carmen* in that city. Opera houses of the status and prestige of that of Vienna have no need to invite disaster by adding to their repertoire an undoubted failure. One asks, then, if the failure of *Carmen* was real or supposed ; if it belongs to legend or to history ; if the treatment meted out to it was of so pronounced a character that it warrants the employment of the word failure, or the word success.

According to Pigot, the first-night audience contained representatives of many aspects of Parisian life and thought. The Paris of litera-ture, of the arts and of society lent support to the new venture.[2] Applause was neither frequent nor vigorous. The prelude to the second act managed, however, to rouse the audience from its lethargy. The toreador's song and the quintet found favour in its eyes. But, by the time the curtain fell, the auditors, who had lapsed into a state bordering on indifference, indulged in only

[1] Henry Gauthier-Villars : *Bizet.*

[2] Vincent d'Indy, however, has it that there were not many composers present. *Vid. inf.*

a temperate demonstration.[1] If some portions had found their way into the public's esteem, others were found wanting. The famous cadence associated with Don José's " *Carmen, je t'aime* " caused flutterings in a few pedantic breasts. Again, there were those who reproached Bizet for his weaknesses, his concessions to bourgeois taste, as exhibited for example in Escamillo's solo. Thus Pigot, whose account of the matter seems to imply that Bizet had fallen between two stools ; he was at once too bold, and too timid to be bold.

The impression made by a work depends upon the music and upon the sensibility of the audience. It depends also upon the interpretation. Before passing to other topics, it might be well to supplement what I have just said with a brief reference to the performance. In spite of his shortcomings, du Locle had something of the artist in him. Every production with which he had anything to do benefited from the care and attention that he bestowed upon it. Even Saint-Saëns, who called him the most fantastic director that ever existed, gave him credit for having mounted *Carmen* to perfection. " *Distribution, mise en scène,*" he

---

[1] It may be well to set down what Henri Rochefort said in *Le Figaro* of 2nd January 1908 : " On the evening of the first performance, *Carmen* was hissed to such an extent that one could hardly hear the mention of the authors' names." After quoting these words, Gauthier-Villars tells us that this is an exaggerated statement : " There was never any uproar, but the audience remained unmoved and bored. . . . The public showed its customary disdain towards him [Bizet], and the opera dragged out a mediocre existence."

wrote, " all was irreproachable. Du Locle was an artist, and what he did, he did well."[1] As we shall see, the suggestion was made that du Locle, who could not understand this " Cochin-Chinese music," did not wish *Carmen* to succeed ; but, not desiring to be reproached on this score, he produced it with scrupulous care. For instance, a serious attempt was made to provide the various singers with costumes which had the rare merit of historical exactitude. The appearance of dragoons carrying lances provoked discussion, as a result of which the sceptical learned that in 1824, Spanish dragoons did actually carry these weapons. The orchestra, it is said, bore its part well, except for a hitch when the player of the big drum, losing count of his bars, entered brutally at a pianissimo.[2] Lack of unanimity and insufficiency of rehearsal combined to make the chorus less satisfactory ; and, a point to be noticed in these days, some of its members did not smoke their cigarettes without bad effect.

The cast was as follows :

CARMEN	...	...	...	...	Mme. GALLI-MARIÉ
MICAELA	...	...	...	...	„ CHAPUY
FRASQUITA	...	...	...	...	„ DUCASSE
MERCÉDÈS	...	...	...	...	„ CHEVALIER
DON JOSÉ	...	...	...	...	M. LHÉRIE
ESCAMILLO	...	...	...	...	„ BOUHY
LE DANCAÏRE	...	...	...	...	„ POTEL
LE REMENDADO		...	...	...	„ BARNOLT

[1] *L'Art du Théâtre*, January 1905.
[2] Pigot.

Morales	...	...	...	...	M. Duvernoy
Zuniga	...	...	...	...	„ Dufriche
Lillas Pastia		...	...	...	„ Nathan

Of the singers the most outstanding was undoubtedly Mme Galli-Marié, whose reading of the part allotted to her possessed fire, life, and exuberant vitality ; in fact, she did not escape censure on the score of excessive realism. " Mme Galli-Marié seems to take pleasure in accentuating the unlovely aspect of this dangerous rôle," said *Le Gaulois.*[1] While her vocal powers do not appear to have been astounding, there can be no doubt that she possessed temperament and a real ability to invest with interest the parts she undertook.

But the voice of protest did not lack a greater theme with which it might create much stir. In a moment of quite wonderful illumination some clever person discovered that *Carmen* could not be defended on moral grounds. We are all aware that Doctor Samuel Smiles did not write the libretto ; we are all aware that Lillas Pastia's tavern was not a family hotel ; we have all made the acquaintance of the unlovely characters who inhabit the pages of Mérimée. What we were ignorant of was the squeamishness of the habitués of the Opéra Comique. Here, surely, is food for Momus ; here a circumstance that calls for the pen of a Juvenal or a Swift. The charge has been laid at the feet of no less a personage than du

[1] 6th March 1875.

Locle, the person in all Paris whose interest it was to see the opera succeed. By way of substantiation, Pigot relates how a minister wrote to the director asking for a box for the first night. In his reply, du Locle requested the minister's attendance at the *répétition générale*, because, in view of its nature, it was advisable for him to judge whether *Carmen* were a piece which his family ought to hear. If this charge of immorality is not double-dyed hypocrisy, all one can say is that the mentality of Paris has undergone a violent change ; that opera-goers all over the world are a debased race (even though the temperature of the original libretto is higher than that of any probable English translation) ; and that those who patronised some of the Italian works which preceded *Carmen* were conveniently deaf, dumb, and blind. A work is not more moral because the exploits of characters, whom one would not care to introduce to one's sister, are sung in saccharine thirds and sixths. Carmen is not by any reckoning a lady, nor are the smugglers gentlemen. But it so happens that many operatic characters are in the same category. Is there no cause for complaint in Mozart's *Marriage of Figaro* or *Don Juan* ? Is Lucrezia Borgia a paragon of all the virtues ? What is one to say of the Duke of Mantua who struts through *Rigoletto* ? Has it not been remarked time and again that Beethoven's Leonora is almost unique in opera by reason of her sublime unselfishness and nobility of heart ?

64

The public drawn to the Opéra Comique was, it has been said, attuned to the quiet emotions of the older works to be heard there. Allowing for this, one is still left astonished. Had those easily distressed habitués placed a large and representative portion of French literature upon a home-made index ? It would seem as if all the prudery of Paris had been swept, as with a broom, into the auditorium of the theatre.

One asks, very naturally, how the composer accepted the verdict of the audience on which so much depended. At the end of the first act, a group of young musicians, among whom was Vincent d'Indy, met Bizet outside the theatre and praised what they had heard. To them he observed : " You are the first who have said that, and I fancy you will be the last." In a little brochure, Hugues Imbert recounts a meeting with Bizet in the wings of the theatre after the performance had just finished. Imbert thought he ought to offer his congratulations on the success of *Carmen*. "Success," answered Bizet quickly, " do you not see that these bourgeois have not understood a blessed word of the work I have written for them ? " What he said, adds Imbert, was unhappily true ; *Carmen* was not understood at its début.[1] Elsewhere, Bruneau recalls the story of Bizet's distress on this eventful evening : " We have been shown Georges Bizet coming out of the Théatre Favart on the night of

[1] Hugues Imbert : *Georges Bizet*.

the 3rd—4th March, 1875, and wandering about
Paris distracted on the arm of Ernest Guiraud, a
terrified witness of his despair and his tears. I
do not know if this intimate and poignant tragedy
is true, but, in any case, I do not doubt the sufferings that the poor man had to endure, sufferings
which at the end of three months got the better
of his energy and courage, and killed him."[1]
Galabert, whom one would expect to have known
what actually happened, thought it possible that
Bizet, coming away from the theatre, suffered
from a passing depression, though on this matter
Guiraud kept silent ; nor did Guiraud speak to
him of the reputed walk through Paris during the
night, in the course of which Bizet was presumed
to have given vent to his feelings.[2] Galabert did,
however, direct his reader's attention to the
testimony of Ludovic Halévy, who wrote : " We
lived at the same house, Bizet and I . . .
we returned by foot in silence. Meilhac accompanied us."[3] This seems to dispose of the story
of the walk with Guiraud. In another place,
Ludovic Halévy tells how he had seen Bizet
reading the criticisms of *Carmen* :[4] " He was
certainly saddened, but not discouraged." A
further picture is left to us by Louis Gallet.
Gallet had written a libretto, *Geneviève de Paris,*

---

[1] *Musica*, February 1905.
[2] Galabert's Introduction.
[3] *Le Théâtre*, January 1905.
[4] Ludovic Halévy: Preface to Louis Gallet's *Notes d'un
Librettiste.*

BIZET

at Bizet's desire.   He wanted to see the composer
in connection with this shortly before his departure for the country.   He found him a little cast
down, smiling a sad smile, but full of ardour at
the thought of his new task.   Bizet spoke at
length of his past sufferings, and his dreams of the
future.[1]

Djamileh had been, as its composer asserted,
passionately discussed.   Critical pens worked
more furiously on its successor ; so furiously,
indeed, that one finds in the lines they wrote a
perverse tribute to the music.   Surely, so much
ink would never have been spilt over an opera that
did not matter.   If popularity may sometimes be
stigmatised as an insult, hissing may often be
construed as an act of homage.   The worst that
can befall an artist is not hostility, but apathy.
For a work to be found disagreeable may not be
flattering to its creator ; it, nevertheless, presumes
the possession of definite attributes on his part.
To be so lacking in these attributes that no man
troubles to express either admiration or detes-
tation is tragedy indeed.   And so it should not
be overlooked that *Carmen* caused a violent
fluttering in the musical dovecotes of Paris.   If
passionate discussion faithfully describes the controversy born of *Djamileh*, a phrase more pungent
must be drawn upon to describe the controversy
born of *Carmen*.   When reading the press notices
Bizet was saddened, but not discouraged.   Let us

[1] Louis Gallet, *Notes d'un Librettiste.*

turn to some of them in order to discover what the critics of the day had to say.

To the critic of *Le Temps* the music did not seem original : " Now the music has verve and character, now it attests more to technical knowledge (*connaissances du métier*) than to invention." The women's chorus of the first act was put down as mediocre. Bizet's imitation of Spanish airs did not impart the least local colour to the work.

La Presse sounded a slightly warmer note. It considered that the opera possessed a high interest, and, in view of the careful workmanship exhibited in it, prophesied its acceptance at the hands of the musicians ; though the writer doubted whether the public which supported the Opéra Comique would find it so much to its taste. " Its greatest merit is knowledge, but inspiration is rare : the melodic phrase is short, broken, so to say, and held together with difficulty. The music of *Carmen* has all the qualities and all the faults of the preceding works by M. Georges Bizet ; from the point of view of the theatre it is neither better nor worse than that of *Les Pêcheurs de Perles*, *La Jolie Fille de Perth*, or *Djamileh*."

In contrast are the words penned by Oscar Commettant in *Le Siècle :*

" . . . It is not, however, by ingenious orchestral touches, bold dissonances or instrumental finesse that one is able to express the low-down rage of Mlle. Carmen, and the aspirations of the outcasts who form her retinue. . . . M. Bizet, who has nothing to learn of what can be learnt, has unhappily still much to divine of what cannot be taught. A little blasé by contact with dissonance and research, his heart needs to recover its musical purity. He thinks too much and he does not feel enough, and his inspirations, even the happiest, lack sincerity and naïveté, that delicious perfume of all artistic production which is so often worth more than all the science in the world. M. Bizet has not yet found his true path. He will attain his ambition, let us hope, but he will have to *unlearn* many things before becoming a dramatic composer."

Perhaps, after all, Gauthier-Villars has sanction for describing this pontiff as "the ineffable Oscar Commettant."

Ernest Reyer, who expressed his views in *Le Journal des Débats*, emerges well from the ordeal imposed by the passing of half a century. He is quite definite in the line he takes up, and reasonably enthusiastic. Nothing could be straighter or more emphatic than the following :

"M. Bizet is a past master in the art of orchestration, and no one knows better the secret of fine harmony and suitable scoring. I already said this to him *à propos* of *Djamileh* and *à propos* of *L'Arlésienne*, which is a jewel ; I may as well repeat it *à propos* of *Carmen.*"

Something of the same nature was expressed in *Le Courrier de Paris*, where the opera was called an "*opéra-tragi-comique* " :

"The music of *Carmen* is light ; it does not attempt to shun melody, and one does not perceive in it any aversion to the recognised usages ; this work is one of those which redound to the credit of a musician."

In the *Monitor Universelle* Paul de Saint-Victor wrote :

" M. Bizet belongs to this new set, whose doctrine consists of allowing the musical idea to evaporate instead of expressing it in definite contours. For this school of which M. Wagner is the oracle . . . a theme is out of fashion, melody superannuated ; the voice, suppressed and dominated by the orchestra, is only a feeble echo. Such ideas must necessarily produce confused works. . . . The orchestration of *Carmen* abounds in clever combinations, and new and rare effects. But the excessive opposition which the voice finds in the instruments is one of the errors of the new school."

The representative of *Le Gaulois* regretted that, while Bizet had undoubted talent and complete erudition, he lacked the melodic raciness which flowed from the pens of Auber, Adam, Herold and Boieldieu :

" Altogether a curious libretto, creditable music, adequate interpretation, such is my impression of the new piece, about which there has been too much talk."

Finally, *L'Illustration* thought that while the libretto was one of the most taking that had been heard at the Place Favart, it demanded the co-operation of a musician out of the common, instead of a musician like Bizet, a man of talent who had never shown either suppleness of imagination nor brilliance.

All these judgments have some interest and, perhaps, some historical value, but one of the brightest pieces of work executed by the critics of the time has not yet been mentioned, and in view of its character it is hardly surprising that Gauthier-Villars should have given it some prominence. The critic of *La France*, speaking of the air sung by Don José in the wings, condemned its lack of contour and its pretentious harmony. After quoting this extraordinary verdict, Gauthier-Villars points out that the number in question is precisely the only one which Bizet has written without accompaniment.

One returns to the question : Was *Carmen* a failure, or was it only called a failure ? If it were a failure, why should Arthur Pougin call one of his articles *The Legend of the Failure of Carmen and the Death of Bizet*; and why should Gabriel Bernard, writing in *Musica* for June, 1912, speak of *The Legend of the Non-Success of Carmen* ? Do not such activities imply both that a widespread belief in its non-success existed and that this belief had no sure foundation in fact ? One prosecutes the inquiry in the hope that, amid the jarring notes and discordant voices, one may find something resembling the truth. For, be it understood, the theme of *Carmen*, its production and reception, did not exhaust itself on the pale dawn which followed the *première*.

First let me deal with an article entitled " The One Thousandth Performance of *Carmen*," which appeared in *Le Théâtre* for January, 1905. It came from the pen of Ludovic Halévy, who was likely to have a full knowledge of what happened. He was one of the librettists. As such, he would be brought into close contact with Bizet and the others who launched the opera, and it is a fair conjecture that he had a key to every seeming problem connected with that delicate operation. Being one of those directly responsible for the work, he did not require to rely upon the testimony which someone's aunt gave to a friend's cousin. He stood, so to speak, inside the ring. What he says, while it will amply repay study by all attracted to the story, is too long to be quoted here. It must, consequently, suffice to fix upon some of the most essential features of a narrative that certainly seems to throw light upon the question of which it treats.

To begin with, Halévy recalls three historic dates—that of the first performance under the direction of du Locle, the 3rd of March, 1875 ; that of the first revival under the direction of Carvalho, the 21st of April, 1883 ; and that of the second revival also under the direction of Carvalho, the 27th of October, 1883, which the writer calls the last and decisive. From 1870 to 1874 the directors of the Opéra Comique were de Leuven and du Locle. Never, says Halévy, was an association more singular, bizarre and discordant. After giving an indication of the accomplishments of the two men in order to show the differences which existed between them, the writer speaks out boldly. Without du Locle *Carmen* would not have been brought out at the Opéra Comique in 1875. Two years earlier Bizet had been convinced that Mérimée's novel

offered material for operatic treatment. Meilhac
and Halévy shared this view, as did du Locle
when Halévy spoke to him of the project. But,
not sure of his colleague, who would be shocked at
such a subject, the director deputed Halévy to
tackle de Leuven. Forthwith Halévy set out on
his perilous errand. The story of his reception
lacks nothing of brightness or humour. Hardly
had the well-intentioned missionary opened his
mouth than de Leuven burst out :

" . . . The *Carmen* of Mérimée ! . . . Is it
not she who is assassinated by her lover ? . . .
And this company of thieves, gypsies and cigarette
makers ! . . . At the Opéra Comique ! . . .
the family theatre ! . . . You would put our
public to flight. . . . It is impossible ! "

Halévy argued and explained. The librettists
had introduced into the piece a young girl of true
opéra-comique pattern ; the gypsies were not
without their humorous traits, and if there were a
death, inevitable to the dénouement, it came at
the end of an act in which there was much animation and brilliance—an act played under a blue
sky, on a fête day, with processions, a ballet and
fanfares. After holding out stubbornly, de Leuven
at last succumbed, but dismissed his visitor with
the weighty admonition ; he must not introduce
a death at the final scene. Such an end had
never been witnessed at the Opéra Comique.
Six months after, de Leuven resigned, owing,
Halévy believed, in some measure to anxiety

over the presentation of so revolutionary an
opera.

The rehearsals began in December, 1874, and
at once difficulties arose. While the principal
singers worked themselves into their parts, the
chorus gave serious trouble ; its members
threatened to go on strike. After a couple of
months devoted to study, some of them found
two of the chorus pieces in the first act to be impossible of execution—the entrance of the cigarette makers and the hubbub after the arrest of
Carmen. It may be conceded that the music
was somewhat removed from that which the
chorus of the Opéra Comique had usually to sing.
Halévy, however, makes it quite clear that the
source of the trouble lay not alone in the music,
but partly in the actions to be carried out by the
stage crowd. The interpretation of such pieces
meant more than the mere singing of them. One
had to move, to stir, to express surprise and
interest, and of this the placid traditions of the
house knew nothing. The chorus had been
accustomed to stand in a line and fix its gaze upon
the conductor. An objection to some of the
writing, on the score of its impracticability, arose
also with the orchestra, but the instrumental
material must have been superior to the vocal.
At least, Halévy chronicles that, after rehearsals
somewhat more frequent than usual, the musicians
managed to play the unplayable.

Hope ran high as the time for production drew

near. At the final rehearsal the music, particularly that of the fourth act, thrilled those who heard it. Altogether, Bizet's friends anticipated a good reception, even if, on the *morning* of the *première*, two or three prominent papers contained cutting remarks on the new work, whose production was to signalise the end of the Opéra Comique as a family theatre ; a deplorable piece of conduct this, because, as Halévy says caustically, the state gave the Opéra Comique a subvention partly in order to provide a theatre of this kind. Hopes, fears, and doubts were soon to be laid to rest, however.

The evening came and brought with it two dramas, one on the stage and the other in the auditorium. Halévy wrote to a friend an account of what happened. As he composed his letter on the day following the *première*, the impression made upon him could not have become dim, nor could his memory very well have played him false. Here is the report which he submitted :

"The first act went well. The entrance of Galli-Marié was applauded. . . . Applause for the duet of Micaela and Don José. Splendid finish to this act . . . applause and recalls . . . a large number of people on the stage at the fall of the curtain. . . . Bizet surrounded and congratulated . . . The second act less fortunate. The opening very brilliant. The entrance of the toreador produced a great effect. Then coldness. . . . From that point Bizet departing more and more from the traditional form of the *opéra-comique*, the public was surprised, embarrassed and perplexed. . . . Fewer people round Bizet during the interval. Felicitations less sincere, awkward, and constrained. The coldness increased with the third act. . . . The only applause on the part of the public was for the air of Micaela, an air in the ancient, classic style. . . . Still fewer people on the stage. And after the fourth act, which was received with icy coldness from the beginning to the end, no one . . . save three or four faithful friends of Bizet. They all had comforting words upon their lips, but sadness in their eyes. *Carmen* had not succeeded."

After reminding his readers that, with few exceptions, the press was very severe, Halévy proceeds to point out that three numbers of the score did not depart from the usual *opéra-comique* manner—the duet for Micaela and Don José in the first act, the toreador's song in the second, and Micaela's song in the third. Significantly enough, the audience applauded them. Had Bizet cast the remainder of his work in this style, he would probably have gained a great success ; but, for the rest, he wished his music faithfully to reflect the passion, movement, and life of the plot. He sought music that should spring from the action, intensify it, and find its justification by so doing ; music that should have nothing in common with conventional opera and its openings for applause. His adoption of this line troubled the first-night house by taking it out of its habitual environment. One of the best portions of the score, the duet for Carmen and Don José at the end of the last act, passed completely unnoticed.

Not unnaturally, Halévy turns to some of the press verdicts, and thereafter relates how *Carmen*

struck " le père " Dupin. The story is too good
to be left untold, if only because Dupin himself,
while a character, may also have represented a
certain type of music-lover. This gentleman was
born in 1791. In 1808 he presented a little piece
at the Vaudeville, a forerunner of some two hundred theatrical productions of a light character.
During his career he had collaborated with Scribe,
whom he set upon a pedestal. Meilhac and
Halévy counted him among their friends, and he
came every afternoon to Meilhac's house in order
to play billiards. Although eighty-four years of
age when *Carmen* appeared, he was still capable of
enthusiasm, as he showed by being present at the
première. The next day he arrived as usual, but
irritated and wrathful, and at once he launched
out vehemently upon his two friends.

" Yesterday I was at the Opéra Comique," he
said. " I won't mince matters with you. . . .
Your *Carmen* is a failure, an utter failure. It will
not be played twenty times. . . . There are
three pieces in it which contain music, and make
some effect because *they come to an end*. As for
the others, my goodness, they never finish. There
is not even an opening for applause. That's not
music. . . . And your piece is not a piece. . . .
There is a man who meets a woman . . . he
finds her beautiful, and that's the first act. . . .
He loves her and she loves him, and that's the
second. She does not love him any more, and
that's the third. . . . He kills her, that's the

fourth. And you call that a piece ! In a true
piece there ought to be surprises, happenings,
incidents, things that make you say, ' What is
going to occur in the next act ? ' That is the
real theatre ! Reread the pieces of Scribe !
There is nothing better. You pretend that you
have done well by the national genre, the *opéra-
comique* . . . it is a crime . . . do you hear ?
A crime l ''

Flustered or not, Dupin returned to the source
of his irritation. He even saw the three hundredth
performance, much to his own astonishment.[1]

Having disposed of the first night, Halévy
speaks of the later fortunes of the opera. The
performances continued and were not, as has been
said, given to empty houses. Generally speaking,
the receipts exceeded those of other pieces in the
repertoire. Gradually the circle of admirers
increased.

In 1876 du Locle resigned, and his successor
was Carvalho. To Halévy, Carvalho repeated all
the stale platitudes about the riskiness of the plot.
He admired some of the numbers, but the opera
as a whole did not meet the needs of his public,
and he would have nothing to do with it. The
attitude of Paris had not, of course, been without
its influence. A piece so dangerous could not
hope to gain a footing in the French provinces.
While this deadlock continued in France, *Carmen*
made its bow beyond the frontiers. As has been

[1] This took place in 1887.

said above, Vienna took it up. It was first played there on the 23rd of October, 1875, and owed much of its success to the lavishness with which it was mounted. In its journey South it underwent a transformation. The corps de ballet of the Opera appeared in the last act, where a divertissement from *La Jolie Fille de Perth* was interpolated, and no pains were spared to make the procession of toreros a feast for the eye. Halévy describes the Viennese version as an *opéra-ballet*. A new feature lay in the recitatives provided by Guiraud, which superseded the dialogue. Brussels followed hard upon the heels of Vienna by giving the opera on the 3rd of February 1876, when, according to the librettist, it won a decisive success. In 1878 it at last found a home in the French provinces. Halévy again sought out Carvalho, who, of course, knew of these provincial activities. This time the director felt disposed to put on the opera—but could not find a Carmen.

Yes, Galli-Marié had been admirable, only she had played the part too realistically. Carvalho's search lasted for four years. Then, suddenly, he announced that *Carmen* would be played. The explanation which Halévy gives of this unexpected change of front is singular. The director's existence had become a positive burden to him. Not only the admirers of Bizet, but theatre-goers, critics, ministers of state called as with one voice : " When are we to hear *Carmen* ? "

The rehearsals commenced, and while, in Halévy's view, a month's further preparation was necessary in order to do the work full justice, Carvalho abruptly intimated that the opera would be restored to the repertoire in eight days. He himself considered the piece ready for production. Halévy contested this. The first two acts were certainly ready ; the third was scarcely ready ; and the fourth not at all.

On the 21st of April 1883, *Carmen* saw its second *première*, if the bull be permitted. The first and second acts came off victoriously. Those who had listened to them eight years earlier rubbed their eyes. Where was the obscurity, where the difficulty ? Those who had not heard them previously were equally astounded, for they understood, nay, enjoyed, this music. When the third act began the audience thought that it had, by some mischance, dropped into a rehearsal. The singers, who were not at home in their parts, knew neither their words nor the stage business as they should have known them, nor did they fare better in the last scene. Murmurs of dissatisfaction arose from the front. In fear, Halévy and his friends wondered if this unfortunate piece had not suffered. Carvalho did not escape censure, but the press acclaimed the opera as a masterpiece, and the receipts gladdened the managerial heart. The director, on his part, owned to his error. Later in the same year he announced a revival. On the 27th of October,

1883, *Carmen* filled the bill of the Opéra Comique, and with unfeigned pleasure the Parisian public hailed the return of Galli-Marié, the heroine of the first night. The evening proved to be one of such overwhelming success that it vindicated those who had believed in the opera from the start, as it vindicated the composer of that opera.

Ludovic Halévy was, as I have said, one of the actors of the drama. Galli-Marié was another, and she, too, gave her views concerning *Carmen* and its reception in an interview which took place at Nice twenty-eight years after the event in question.[1]

" No," the singer is reported to have said, " *Carmen* did not collapse after a few performances. The truth is that the work had a bad press—a very bad press. Certain critics were shocked because, for the first time, or almost for the first time, a piece came to a tragic conclusion at the Opéra Comique, where the immemorial tradition was that the tenor and the first soprano married one another at the end of the last act. . . . Of course, you know that since *Carmen* crimes of passion are common in our second state-supported theatre."

" Then," asked the interviewer, " *Carmen* held the bill in the first instance ? "

" We have played it about forty times," answered Galli-Marié, " and the public was always very appreciative."

The singer went on to speak of the libretto,

considered from the standpoint of Mérimée's book.

"Speaking without the least desire to be critical, I may say that the operatic *Carmen* is far removed from the quasi-realistic conception of the novel. From a literary point of view she is, without doubt, less interesting, but one can hardly disregard the difficulty which Meilhac and Halévy had to dispose of in order to construct a dramatic theme capable of musical development. The poetical atmosphere of the work, even its idealistic atmosphere, if one may say so, has, above all, been the work of the musician."

It will be observed that in her recital the singer ranged herself on the side of those who attributed much to the horror with which some people contemplated the tragic finish. The Opéra Comique did not permit such a scene. To ring down the curtain upon a gypsy just done to death by a crazy outlaw, upon whom the dread arm of the law falls, was, perhaps, to outrage tradition and fly in the face of all things right and reasonable. But, without incurring the reproach of captiousness, one may question whether the power and sanctity of tradition alone explained the temper of the protest. The cult of the happy ending has never lacked devotees. Thackeray, for example, disliked books which closed on a sombre note ; he could not bring himself to reread *The Bride of Lammermoor* or *Kenilworth*, because " the end is unhappy, and people die, and are murdered."

The preference for a bright and optimistic conclusion is creditable, I doubt not, to the heart of
humanity. Most people enjoy a pleasurable sensation when they find that the nursemaid is to be
married to the young nobleman, and will dispense
hospitality in a high hall with oaken rafters.
They love to see the problem of the lost heir solved
and the poor neglected lad installed in the ances-
tral mansion, much to the chagrin of the dark-
whiskered adventurer, who decamps to Boulogne.
Having wept over the beautiful tale of the struggling author and his trusting wife, they applaud
the telegraph boy who bears the news that Uncle
Robert has died in San Francisco leaving Jack that
little gold mine of his. This popular attitude
is capable of psychological explanation. Most
people would rather be happy than sad ; they
would read, or see rather what ministers to their
high spirits than what stimulates them to thought ;
they prefer agreeable fictions to disagreeable
truths. More than this, they get, at second-
hand, something of the justice which the world
seems to deny them. The girl, reading of the
country lass who becomes a duchess, unconsciously suggests to herself the possibility of becoming a duchess ; does she read her book with
the utmost glamour and excitement, she already
sees a Lohengrin, symbol of romance and deliver-
ance, at her own side. We all feel more or less
that many people who inhabit the byways and
backwaters of life deserve a better fate. We all

feel that many exalted personages little deserve
their exaltation. And the raising of the obscure,
the virtuous, and the simple at the expense of the
eminent, the unworthy, and the sophisticated, be
it never so crude, will always strike a large number
of people as something like poetic justice. So far
as I know, there is nothing to show that the cult
of the happy ending was less popular in the France
of 1875 than it is in many quarters to-day. There
appears to be considerable evidence that it had a
distinct vogue, and I fancy that the objection
taken to the end of *Carmen* lay not wholly in its
defiance of custom, but in the personal detesta-
tion with which a large section of the public
viewed it.

De Leuven advised Ludovic Halévy to be done
with the killing. Obviously, this was as easy to
say as it would have been difficult to carry out.
The entire opera moves steadily towards this
dreadful calamity. The fates have, in Æschylean
manner, to be appeased. One wonders what the
protestants said about the scene in which Carmen
and the two cigarette girls read their futures in
the cards. As this does not indicate a happy
ending, its excision, or revision, would have been
necessary ; neither alternative to be lightly regarded or undertaken. There are hints and pre-
monitions, which likewise become meaningless
unless the end is tragic. Change the end, the
entire edifice collapses. I do not know what the
objectors desired. They were destructive, in so

84

far as they denounced a death. They were not constructive, in that they left unspoken a possible alternative. Without feeling that they outraged commonsense and all those qualities which go to make a work artistic, could they have looked upon one of the possible-impossible makeshifts ? Could they have looked complacently upon Don José leading Carmen to the altar, with Escamillo as a fashionably attired groomsman ; or upon Escamillo leading Carmen to the altar, while Don José, the true lover, staggered out into the black night to carry a secret sorrow to the grave ? And what solution, other than those absurd expedients. presents itself ? If a section of the public did not wish to see a murder and an arrest, it was at liberty to employ its leisure elsewhere. It had the right to take exception to both of these unfortunate occurrences, but we are not thereby denied the right to say what we think of its intelligence.

In his book called *The Prima Donna*, Sutherland Edwards states that, according to the original plan, Carmen was to have been represented as capable of remorse, and, that after the card scene, she was to have had the stage to herself in order to express her emotions in a pathetic air. If this means that a happy ending was in contemplation, I, for one, can only rejoice that such a proposal was abandoned. A Carmen capable of remorse is no Carmen for me ; and, be it observed, unless the opera were drastically overhauled, a Carmen capable of remorse would be an inconsistent

Carmen. Why the authors discarded the scheme, if such were in mind, Sutherland Edwards does not make quite clear. He speaks of this scheme as having been worked out for Marie Roze, but surely some more powerful influence than the substitution of Galli-Marié must have been active In any case, we can never be too thankful that, if the happy ending were seriously considered, the superior one prevailed.

As for tradition, it needs to be said that one can render this deity excessive tribute, even in France. If, on account of its final scene, *Carmen* is not an *opéra-comique*, then it is not. The fact may cause purists to place the opera in another category, which activity will not alter a semiquaver of it ; it may cause some people to emulate George Stephenson and say : " So much the worse for *opéra-comique*." It is well to bear in mind that force of circumstances sometimes insists upon our coming to grips with tradition. At those moments one asks how far loyalty to it is justified, nay, how far it is profitable. To take a certain mould, place new works in it, and praise or denounce them according as they fit, or do not fit, that mould is perhaps to do service to tradition. The zeal may become excessive. *Carmen* did not fit the mould, therefore *Carmen* was not an *opéra-comique*, which was to be proved. This is very simple, and to some minds conclusive ; to others, more questioning, it raises a query. Does a mould never become antiquated ; if a work re-

fuses to fall within its confines, is it not possible
we may be mistaken in calling its apparent re-
calcitrance a defect ?   Much of the past denuncia-
tion of works, which is to us incomprehensible,
has its roots in the application of an out-moded
measure.   Of this particular case, I would simply
say that anyone is at liberty to deny *Carmen's* right
of entry to the company of *opéras-comiques* if he so
wills ; just as anyone is at liberty to declare that
it enlarged the domain of the *opéra-comique* at a
time when it required enlarging.   But the pro-
hibition need not stifle admiration of *Carmen* as a
work of art.   Since 1875 tragic happenings have
taken place on the stage of the Opéra Comique.
Laparra's *La Habanera* has been played there.
The Seine has not caught fire, nor have the heavens
fallen.   In other words, a new tradition has been
created, which will in no wise lack defenders
worthy of their sires.

I return to history with a curious reference to
Carmen, which is to be encountered in a volume
called *My Memories*, written by Ovide Musin, the
well-known Belgian violinist.   Musin lived in
Paris at the time *Carmen* was being rehearsed, and
he informs us that he attended the last rehearsals
with Bizet, who made his observations from a
corner of the balcony.   What he writes is to me
tantalising.   He whets, but does not entirely
satisfy, my appetite for information.   Musin read
many of the criticisms and comments on what he
calls the " failure and success " of *Carmen* without

discovering in them a satisfactory reason for the failure and success. This he attributes to the omission of some important details. " I have been in a position," he writes, " by my relation [*sic*], to know the inside cause of this failure which caused the premature death of the genial composer, Bizet." According to Musin, the orchestra was perfect, the chorus well trained, and nothing left undone which could make the production one of the greatest successes ever seen at the Opéra Comique. He traces the failure to a certain portion of the second act, which did not altogether please the bourgeois patrons of the house. " It was circulated about like wildfire that the opera was indecent, and that the second act took place in a disreputable quarter of the city. This was enough to keep whole families away, and at the fifth performance the box-office receipts were so poor and the failure of the opera so pronounced that Bizet succumbed to the crushing disappointment a few months later."[1] The opera-going public, he observes, was not so scrupulous when it went to hear Gounod's *Faust*, Rubinstein's *Nero*, and Massenet's *Hérodiade*. Musin speaks thereafter of the Brussels reception of the opera, of the singers who appeared at the first performance in Paris, and of the habanera. It will be seen that he does not throw more light on the matter than some other writers, and, in view of his being in a position to know the inside causes of the failure,

[1] *Cf.* Ludovic Halévy on this question of the receipts.

one regrets the scantiness of his comments. It
will not pass unobserved that he found the chorus
satisfactory.

I propose now to augment what has been set
down here by giving the views of one or two
eminent musicians on the topic which has engaged
the reader's attention. Some pages of *L'Art du
Théâtre* for January, 1905, were devoted to a
symposium on the work of Bizet, to which both
Vincent d'Indy and Saint-Saëns contributed. In
d'Indy's view *Carmen* proved the point of departure for the evolution of dramatic music in
France. " The work was," he declares, " a new,
bold experiment, that is why (it is in the nature of
things) it did not obtain any success." In his
Life of César Franck d'Indy speaks contemptu-
ously of the students of composition who " accused
this work of excessive Wagnerism, while others
turned away their eyes from so coarse a subject
and cried ' Fie ! ' at the top of their voices."

Happily I am able to supplement the foregoing
with a letter touching upon the first night, which
the same commentator has very kindly allowed me
to reproduce. His letter, I ought to add, was
written *au courant de la plume*, and without
thought of publication.

"I attended the first performance of *Carmen*," he says,
" when I was still a pupil of the organ class at the Conservatoire,
which Bizet liked and attended regularly. He had reserved
two tickets to be drawn by lot among the pupils of the class.
Fate favoured me, along with my comrade Camille Benoit,
and I will always remember with emotion the feeling of a

new art which overcame us from the beginning until the end of the piece. Only a long time after did I feel this emotion again, at the first performance of *Pélleas et Mélisande*.

At the first interval, both of us, enraptured, went in search of Bizet in order to thank him and tell him of our joy; we found him walking about gloomily with Hartmann, the publisher, in the Rue Favart, and to our enthusiastic declarations, he replied sadly : ' My dear fellows, you are the first to tell me that . . . and I am afraid you will be the last to-night ! '

The audience, to which we paid scant attention, seemed neither shocked nor astonished but *indifferent ;* obviously these people were bored. Composers who were present (there were not many) were secretly satisfied with the failure, and only later on was it thought of accusing the piece of immorality . . . a very unsuitable piece for furthering the marriage interviews of which the Opéra Comique had a monopoly at the time. All the pupils of the composition class at the Conservatoire let forth their ire against this intruder and started a campaign in the name of offended modesty. I fell out with some of my comrades regarding this matter.

This is the way experiments were treated at that time in Paris. . . . Now, it is the contrary which happens; success favours unimportant productions, bereft of musical feeling, which have come from ignorant composers on behalf of whom a clever advertising campaign has been conducted. *Carmen* which formed a beautiful *musical* work, did not succeed at first . . . and nowadays snobs extol to the skies a work although it contains only *noise*."

As usual, Saint-Saëns does not mince matters. After speaking of the manner in which *Carmen* was prepared, he writes :

" Apart from being entirely reactionary, the criticism of this period was execrable: the piece itself was denounced as indecent, as of a revolting immorality. My duties having prevented me from being present at the first and second performances, I had the opportunity to hear it run down by everyone before I knew it. The music was called operetta music, and more often than not impossible music. I was, however, able to attend the third performance. In coming out of the theatre I strolled into a café to scribble to Bizet : ' I find it remarkable, and I can't but let you know'. This fine work was finely rendered. The contrast between the compelling boldness of Mme. Galli-Marié and the chaste and pure talent of the future Mme. André [1] was perfect. The music was sung as it was written, with a due sense of its rhythmic character."

Saint-Saëns finishes his observations with a reference to the advent of bad traditions. Singers for whom song and music are two different things, he laments, have destroyed the rhythm that is the soul of this Spanish music ; and the public, having approved the work, is enchanted . . . it would be even more so if it could encounter the true *Carmen*, which it previously rejected.

In his volume *La Musique Française*, Alfred Bruneau dwells upon the opera, and the drain it made on Bizet's physical and nervous resources. He sees in *Carmen* the logical continuation of the national traditions, which are therein enlarged.

" Bizet," he continues, " wrote it with his blood and his tears, and made a martyr of himself to bequeath a work vibrant, palpitating, and full of song. . . . Anger died down, truth having gradually carried out its work of peace. The public had to acknowledge that the love story of the soldier and the gypsy, which it had at first declared absolutely incompatible with the nobility of art, is eminently lyrical. . . . All is original, and that explains the long resistance of the public."

[1] The exponent of the part of Micaela.

With the foregoing ought to be bracketed a few words written by Gabriel Fauré : [1]

> "That the story of Mérimée transported to the stage of the Salle Favart should have been able in 1875 to surprise and bewilder a public rooted in habit, that it seemed to conform little to the traditions of the *opéra-comique*, is understandable. But what one cannot understand is that the music of Bizet, so clear, so fresh, so full of colour, sensibility and charm, did not conquer the public from the first moment."

Having lent an ear to so many voices, the reader may not be anxious to listen to another. It would, nevertheless, be wrong to refuse a place to Maurice Lefèvre, over whose name an article devoted to *Georges Bizet, the Musician* appeared in *Musica* for June 1912. I have heard from the lips of one who knew Bizet very well that the restoration of *Carmen* to the Opéra Comique stage owed not a little to a press campaign. Lefèvre's lines corroborate this assertion, and for me, at least, the interest in what he writes centres very largely upon that part of his article which tells how this press campaign began, and how, snowball-like, it increased as it went on. Lefèvre opens in indignant strain.

> "If ever," he says, "I have the honour to be Vice-President of the Association of Musical and Dramatic critics, I will ask a committee to allow me the sum necessary for the placing of a commemorative plaque to the memory of the unhappy and illustrious Georges Bizet, with this expiatory inscription : 'To the victim of musical criticism, to the great musician, misunderstood and scoffed at, killed by disgust and sorrow '."

[1] *Le Figaro*, 24th of December 1904.

He follows up this with references, far from flattering, as will be guessed, to the articles which " finished " *Carmen* and *L'Arlésienne* ; to Félix Clément, the successor of Fétis and compiler of a *Dictionary of Operas* ; and to the crowd of ignorant dilettanti who victimised the composer. With pride he then confesses that he had a hand in the re-establishment of the opera ; this is how it came about.

In 1882, the house of Choudens published the score arranged for piano duet. Every afternoon Lefèvre and a few others met at the house of a young musician, Georges Street by name. André Messager and Raoul Pugno were members of the little coterie, and those two musicians played the opera, repeating time and again the passages found most thrilling by the enthusiastic auditors. *Carmen* was to the select circle of admirers what *The Marriage of Figaro* had been to the Mozart-intoxicated public of Prague. They spoke and thought only of the work. " At that time," observes the writer, with a sly dig at fashionable propriety, " it was not yet bad taste to feel deeply and to express oneself with emphasis."

Lefèvre held a post on the staff of a paper called *Le Clairon*. It was the month of June, and things were not favourable to a journalist hunting for news. Parliament had retired for the recess ; politics offered no material ; there was not even a sensational murder to work up. An entire dearth of copy carried the spirit of depression into those places where men sit and turn out their lines. When things were thus, journalistically speaking, at their lowest ebb, the editor of *Le Clairon* asked Lefèvre to write a criticism of Auber's *Le Maçon*, which was being revived at the Opéra Comique. After the performance, Lefèvre returned to the office, and wrote his notice. At the end of it, he reproached Carvalho with leaving out in the cold a masterpiece like *Carmen*, and wasting time by putting on one of the buffooneries of Auber. The next day several of his journalistic brethren took up the cry, and Lefèvre happily gained editorial commendation for the lead he had given. Not content with this, he proposed to his editor that he should see Carvalho, in order to find out the reason for that gentleman's hostility towards *Carmen*. He made up his mind to see also Meilhac and Halévy, the librettists. His account of these interviews follows. Carvalho rode his old hobby-horse. He could not countenance such a piece at his reputable house. On the second act especially, which shows the posada of Lillas Pastia, he exhausted his vocabulary of vituperation. At the start of the interview he had called Lefèvre "*mon cher enfant*", when it drew to a close he called him "*mon cher monsieur*". As long as he directed the Opéra Comique a low pot-house should not be seen on the stage.

Then came the interviews with Meilhac and Halévy. "Take up *Carmen* !" Lefèvre records them as saying. " Yes, naturally we ask nothing better. But then who is the singer who could assume the part ? "

Lefévre timidly breathed the name of Galli-Marié.

" Oh, whatever you do, don't speak of her", came the reply. " . . . It was she who made the piece fail. . . . Yes, she gave a *too realistic* interpretation. . . Oh yes, there is the book. . . . But there is the opera also. Mme Galli-Marié *played perhaps* the *Carmen* of Mérimée. *She has not played ours.*"

Le Clairon published the material which Lefévre collected—the first occasion, he believed, in which an interview appeared in a Paris paper. The result was amusing. Other sheets reproduced the interviews with strong comments. The question began to assume importance. Parties for and against *Carmen* formed themselves, and their polemics occupied several weeks. At length, a decree from the Opéra Comique intimated that *Carmen* would be produced the following season. With a reference to this reassuring promise and its later fulfilment, Lefèvre's story of his diligence and energy comes to an end.

Before saying anything about the various opinions and comments which I have quoted, it may not be amiss to point out that the question of public taste is not so simple as it appears. It is extremely easy to say that this city is musical, that unmusical. To do so saves a vast amount of trouble, for it frees one from that irksome business, the dealing with minorities and exceptions, however powerful or illustrious ; it relieves one from a mass of detail that is likely to prove intractable material. The difficulty hinted at can best be realised by conning one or two pages of past history. Most people would say, and quite rightly I think, that Vienna has been, and is, one of the most musical cities in the world. I can think of no other city with musical associations more inspiring, of no other city whose inhabitatants have exhibited a deeper love for music, a truer understanding of it, and a greater readiness to acknowledge indebtedness to the masters of the art. But the story of the production of Mozart's *Marriage of Figaro* in Vienna in 1786, tells how the success it won there was short-lived, and did not bear comparison with the more emphatic success it won when produced at Prague shortly after. "Vienna," says Mr E. J. Dent, "had crowded to *Figaro* for a few nights and had probably regarded it rather as a *succès de scandale* ; Prague had shown that it had a real understanding and enthusiasm for Mozart's music."[1]

In a volume called *Vienna and the Austrians*, published in the year 1838, Mrs Frances Trollope, mother of the novelist, wrote of the musical conditions of the Austrian capital, which she had recently visited. I do not know how far Mrs Trollope was fitted to pronounce

[1] E. J. Dent: *Mozart's Operas : A Critical Study.*

judgment upon music and musicians, but in her pages she shows a lively interest in both. She pays a handsome tribute to the Austrian as a music-lover :

> "It cannot be doubted that the love and taste for music is thoroughly genuine and inherent in the Austrian character."

This frank avowal did not, however, cause her to keep silence as to the prevailing taste.

> "Vienna is in truth just now suffering severely from an access of waltzes and rococo. Handel, Mozart, Haydn, and the like are banished from 'ears polite', while Strauss and Lanner rule the hour. Nevertheless, there is no one to whom you can speak on the subject but will utter a very eloquent hymn of praise in honour of the immortal composers. Yet still Strauss and Lanner write and play on, while all the world listens and applauds."

This reminds one of the state of mind of Wagner, when he visited the same city in 1832.

> "What I saw and heard," he records, "edified me little ; wherever I went it was *Zampa* and Straussian pot-pourris on *Zampa*—both, and especially at that time, an abomination to me."

In *Feuersnot* Richard Strauss takes an opportunity of chiding his fellow townsfolk of Munich for their treatment of him, nor does he forget their machinations against Wagner in the sixties. And one might similarly fasten upon several facts relating to Paris, Victor Hugo's " capital of civilisation." How can one do justice to a city where, for so many years, César Franck laboured

97

in the shadows of St. Clotilde ; where, to this day seemingly, there are large numbers of civilised people perfectly content to digest their dinners once a week to the strains of *Faust* and *Samson and Delilah* ? The key to all this is to be found in a very suggestive passage written by Romain Rolland : " . . . . there is not only one Paris ; there are two or three Parises—fashionable Paris, middle-class Paris, intellectual Paris, vulgar Paris —all living side by side, but intermingling very little. If you do not know the little towns within the great Town, you cannot know the strong and often inconsistent life of this great organism as a whole."[1]

Punctilious people will always bear in mind the presence of one of the other Parises ; they will always bear in mind the possible, not to say probable, existence of a thoughtful and dissenting, if not very articulate, minority. Neither will they forget the necessity of exercising what Lord Morley called the historic sense, since few games ask for less skill than the one which consists of throwing mud at our grandfathers. Moreover, they will recognise that, aesthetically speaking, a city, as it is at one moment, differs from itself, as it is at another moment. Psychologists speak of the changes in psychic disposition which manifest themselves in us, and no one needs to be told that while Sachs and Walther typify sanity and progress, the Beckmessers often swagger in

[1] Romain Rolland : *Musicians of To-day.*

98

the limelight. Romain Rolland hints that the simple word Paris represents not merely a large number of people ; it represents a large number of people of varying intelligence, capacity, ambition, and aim. I have made this digression in order to show the difficulties that stand in the way of an accurate appraisal of public taste. The public verdict is the verdict of the majority, the impression made is made by the largest number ; and so, when one speaks glibly of the public, one refers to its dominant characteristic. But the quality, if one dare put it so, of the minority may be of such a nature that history cannot ignore it.

Whether Paris in its general demeanour was, or was not, a musical city in 1875, is a question that does not concern me here. Whether it showed itself to be musical, or unmusical, in its attitude towards *Carmen* is a pertinent question. " All Paris " was at the *première*—all Paris in the sense that every aspect of Parisian life had its representatives. The reception of the opera left something to be desired ; of that, there can, I think, be no doubt. Yet, turning the matter over in one's mind, one hesitates to say that the verdict was unanimous. Call the opera a failure if you will, it returned to the stage eight years later. Should a man be deeply impressed by an opera, he will not forget that opera in eight years ; and, if Lefèvre's account be accurate, it would seem as though only a bold lead were needed to render articulate the thoughts of a not

99

inconsiderable number of people. *Carmen* was never pooh-poohed by Bizet's close friends and staunch admirers. Is it not possible that this small party had adherents of which it knew nothing ? Who is to say how many theatre-goers, little given to making a noise in the world, heard *Carmen*, and admired it ? It is a reasonable conjecture that some of them were only too pleased when the opera reappeared in 1883. But if this be an erroneous conjecture, one has to account for a *volte-face* on the part of the old public—explicable, perhaps, as a reaction generated by the initial impulse—and for the new temper exhibited by the public which had sprung up in the interval. I have no desire to disguise any disappointment suffered by the creators of the piece. As I have said, I wish merely to emphasise the extreme difficulty of dealing with the problem of public taste, and I suggest that, in obscure places, and among people whose views do not commonly sway their fellows, there may possibly have been some perception of *Carmen's* qualities. The many Parises live side by side, but intermingle very little.

After surveying the evidence which has been produced, one ought to be able to arrive at a definite conclusion on several of the questions raised. It is wrong to speak of *Carmen* as a fiasco, unless one stretches that word to fantastic lengths. In the first instance, it had thirty-seven performances, a circumstance which, to my mind,

indicates something better than a failure, even if
one allows for the fact that the sudden withdrawal
of a work spells worry for a theatrical manager,
and for the possibility that, human nature being
what it is, the charge of immorality may have put
a few extra francs into the till after the first night
or two. "With its thirty-seven performances
during the three months of the first season,"
writes Tiersot, "we cannot truly say that it
suffered a defeat ".[1] Gaudier, who takes the
same view, declares categorically that it was
far from being a failure.[2] Both Vienna and
Brussels took it up within a year, which does not
seem to indicate that all those who came in contact
with it regarded it as a work to be cold-shouldered.
Nor do I think it would be possible to name a
day when no one recognised its merits. On the
contrary, one had only to call for *Carmen* at a not
very distant date in order to elicit an enthusiastic
response. I find it difficult to believe that this
response came exclusively from people who had
never heard the opera ; I consider it highly
probably that the response came in fair measure
from some of those who had listened to it in the
past. If the word failure is to be used at all, it
must be used as Hanslick once used it. One
must say that to the majority of those who com-
prised the first-night audience, not to the opera
itself, ought to be applied the derogatory epithet.
That the first-night audience did not fulfil ex-

[1] Julien Tiersot : *Un demi-siecle de Musique Française.*
[2] Charles Gaudier : *Carmen de Bizet.*

pectations is plain. Bizet and his friends anticipated a rapturous welcome ; they looked for spontaneous approval of a score so full of movement, passion, and colour. Such was not forthcoming. Beyond this, one dare scarce venture.

As for the specific objections taken to the work, one is bound to agree that these existed, that they were deep-rooted, and were held by many people. First among them was the prudish objection to the opera, based on moral grounds. On this I have spoken above. Of a kindred nature was the objection to Galli-Marié's too realistic interpretation. It is not, of course, a mark against the work, unless we take the view that the interpretation in question, so far from being a matter of personal caprice, was one imposed upon the artist by the nature of the rôle. The objection to the tragic finish has also been noticed. I have nothing to add to what I have said about it, except that if people encounter something which deeply stirs the very fibre of their being, they will not denounce it because it flies in the face of a theory. I, therefore, take it that those who squealed at the last encounter and its mortal outcome could not have been carried off their feet. They thought more of the *genre opèra-comique* than of the drama enacted before their eyes. The drama could not wean them from their solicitude for a type and tradition. There are always people so preoccupied by the admonition, "Keep off the grass", that they have no eyes for the flowers.

BIZET

And, of course, objections, varying in kind and degree, were levelled at the music itself. The portions which most nearly approached the music ordinarily heard by the Opéra Comique public found more favour than the portions which seemed to tread new ground. It is not easy to see the matter in the light of 1875, because we have become so acclimatized to *Carmen* that we find little, if anything, in it to baffle the intelligence or raise high controversial issues. Not only is this very true. We have heard much music since, and a great fact about musical appreciation often forgotten is that acquaintance with this or that man not only adds to our knowledge, it, unconsciously maybe, modifies our attitude to, and estimate of, that which we have known before. The acquisition of a new fact, the assimilation of a new composer, produces something like an internal dislocation in our artistic selves. Byrd and Weelkes, Purcell and Bach can never be to us, try as we may, exactly what they were to their contemporaries. A work may be admired through the centuries, but the admiration will neither be unvarying in intensity, nor will it spring from an unchanging source. This is because each century makes a contribution to the common good, and because we arrive at a verdict by instituting comparisons. To travel at twenty miles an hour was to travel quickly fifty years ago ; to travel at twenty miles an hour is to travel leisurely to-day. The centuries are in our veins ; we cannot cast

103

our skins ; we cannot throw off that which is an essential part of ourselves. The association of ideas is strong, and we see the single work in relation to the totality of our knowledge. To a man who knows Berlioz, Liszt and Wagner, the Elizabethan composers cannot be what they were to a musician of the " spacious days," because Berlioz, Liszt and Wagner have gone to make the man of to-day what he is. A great deal of the admiration expressed for remote composers is the merest fudge ; a great deal of it comes from people who are as much antiquarians as musicians ; a very modest amount of it is the expression of a genuine musical delight.

If one attempts to hear the music of *Carmen* with a fifty-year-old ear—and it can only be attempt, for the task is humanly impossible—one may, or may not, be able to find in those passages which caused venerable heads to shake, the origins of doubt or of annoyance. To people who knew Rossini and Auber, and the music generally that formed what may be called the common stock of public knowledge, there were passages in the score which need not have caused sleepless nights. One can scarcely credit that the mellifluous duet between Don José and Micaela in the first act troubled the most hidebound reactionary ; nor does it appear to have done so. Of the toreador's song, much the same can be said. And Micaela's solo in the third act is, even from the standpoint of 1875, far from revolutionary. In each of these numbers one discerns a piece of music well written, adequate to the moment, and of a pleasing nature, which may be thoroughly enjoyed without the employment of the higher critical faculty. One does not need to apprentice oneself to it. There is no nut to crack, no technical difficulty to be explained. The melody, carried over the foot-lights, asks for no unusual exertion on the part of the hearer. There is a recognisable theme, which has a recognisable beginning and a recognisable finish—what more could even 1875 have asked for?

The difficulty of dipping into years that were presents itself in a far more acute form when one turns to the passages that fed lively controversy. If it be the case that some people placed a black mark against the prelude because the first part in the key of A major is followed by a second in the key of D minor, one must agree that pedantry held her head very high. While no one is likely to turn a hair at this to-day, it may be well to say that the rightness, or wrongness, of such a proceeding is not to be judged by text-book rules. The result alone is the determining factor. It is quite possible to keep on the safe side of all the text-book rules and produce a work which is not worth the paper it is written on ; it is equally possible to defy those rules and produce a work of precisely the same value. But it is possible to break a rule, and justify the action in the result.

As, without the breaking of rules, there can be no progress, one does not take exception to the action as such. One takes exception to the action only when the result does not seem to justify it ; and it is for the musician to provide the justification. When he does, theorists, taking cognizance of the fact, must amend their theories accordingly. Nothing is more foolish than to imagine that practising musicians are under the slightest obligation to abide by the laws laid down by theorists. Theory is a crystallisation of experience. If this means anything, it means that, by his activity, the composer builds up theory ; it means that the theorist is merely a chronicler. If he is wise he will claim no other office. The place of the theorist is behind, not before, the composer.

It would have been too much to expect many of the conservatives to argue out all this calmly amid the heat and dust of the battle-day. They had evidently their preoccupations, their infallible little footrules with which they confidently measured the musical globe. But the pretty problem of the prelude was not, after all, the only one. Later there were to come strokes that smote them more violently—a modulation at the end of the flower song, for example, which, it is said, assaulted their sensitive ears. One declares that this touch was unusual only to regret the remark, for the music of the past contains many curious things, whose first appearance may easily be credited to others than the originators—can we be quite certain that Liszt has had full credit for all the pioneer work he accomplished ? As the flower song termination does not startle modern musicians, the most to be extracted from any former objection taken to it is that what shocks one generation is not necessarily a source of distress to its successors. For us, indeed, the criticisms passed on the prelude, and the tiny departure from use and wont at the end of Don José's amorous outpouring, are valuable chiefly as an indication of the views held by a section of the Parisian public half a century ago.

Ludovic Halévy indicates that the last two acts fell flat. It will not be forgotten that the third act opens with the chorus, " *Ecoute, écoute, com-pagnons, écoute !* " and that this chorus contains a setting of the words, " *prends garde de faire un faux pas,*" which, I make bold to say, was not couched in the traditional style of *opéra-comique* choruses. Halévy specifically mentions two numbers of the first act which gave the choristers trouble, and necessitated some spontaneous movement on their part, but I fancy that the opening number of the third act must have been, to choristers and auditors alike, more freakish from a musical point of view than any of the choral numbers which preceded it. It may be unwise however, to fix upon this, or that, page to be found in the latter half of the opera ; it may be better to bear in mind that the third and fourth acts failed to carry the audience into ecstacies of delight, and, examining them at our leisure, leave the fact to point its own moral.

It is now time to return to the chief actor in the drama, Bizet himself. He was saddened, but not discouraged. Composers are but human, and, being human, dearly love success. Bizet's mental state arose, I feel sure, from the fact that, having written what he knew to be his best work, he did not take Paris by storm, and it is within the bounds of possibility that he saw only too well how the best parts, the most original parts, of his opera hau not stood so high in the public esteem as had the less original ones. The first night must, undoubtedly, have been a trial for l..m. No sooner had it passed, however, than, according to Halévy, things took a turn for the better. If Bizet's end were hastened by the reception of the work, one must agree that the experience of that first night weighed very heavily upon his spirits ; one must agree also that the impression remained, even after the prospects brightened. This may have been so ; but not, I am convinced, to the extent, or in the manner, commonly believed. It is one thing for a man to be so struck by disappointment that his spirit flickers out and dies ; it is another to be so harassed physically and nervously by the great problems and petty worries incidental to the composing and producing of an opera that the health is seriously affected. Bizet was a temperamental man, and temperamental

men live under a curse.   If they taste the Elysian
joys, they taste also a cup of bitterness never
known to placid folk ; they dwell in both heaven
and hell, while their feet are planted upon earth.
That *Carmen* made heavy draughts upon Bizet's
nervous system will not be gainsaid—Emile
Perrin speaks of the constant work, the excitement
of the rehearsals, the anxieties, the alternating
hopes and fears which undermined his health.[1]
Neither will it be disputed that the first night
tried him sorely.

Yet Bizet, as I see him, was not the kind of
man to go under because Fate frowned upon
him.   If sadness fell upon his brooding spirit,
he had, at least, the compensation known to all
such natures, susceptible as they are to every
change of wind.   I cannot but think that the
loyalty of his friends must have softened the blow ;
I cannot but think that, with all his sensitiveness,
he responded to their words of encouragement.
And we find him, not long after the *Carmen
première*, thinking of new projects.   This scarcely
suggests a man so felled that he is speechless.
It suggests, rather, an indomitable will, a spirit
that takes no denial ; it lends support to Tiersot's
opinion that Bizet did not die of grief.   I would
ask the reader to remember that, the first night
over, things soon improved ; that, before he died,
Bizet knew of the Vienna proposal ; that, as I

[1] Speech at the unveiling of the monument at Père Lachaise,
10th June 1876.

shall try to show, he had never been an extremely robust man ; and that, as he must have observed, the objections taken to *Carmen* were concerned largely with the moral issue, with Galli-Marié's realism, and with the tragic finish, not one of which is a specifically musical objection. So far as I know, there is not a shred of evidence to prove that, had Bizet lived to the age of eighty, he would not have written his *Falstaff*.

Carmen, as we saw, was not long in reaching Vienna and Brussels. I have already recorded the success it attained in the former city, a success that owed not a little to the magnificence of the setting. How the public of Brussels received the novelty may be gathered from a few lines written by Gevaërt in December 1904. They are all the more interesting as Gevaërt had been present when the opera made its bow in the Belgian capital, and as he was not accustomed to surrender himself to gush or flattery. In his statement, he calls to mind the very warm and spontaneous reception accorded to *Carmen* by his countrymen.

"Our public," he says, "is not by nature very demonstrative, but its musical sense is singularly acute, in addition to which, and in the present connection this does not seem to me a matter of indifference—*it knows how to listen without talking*. Ever since that memorable *première Carmen* has enjoyed uninterrupted favour, dropping out of the repertoire of the Monnaie Theatre only to reappear soon. The Bruxellois can pride themselves—as they do—upon being the first to recognise the high value of the work which has conquered, not the crowd alone, but even the superman, Nietzsche himself."

Remembering the place of dispatch, Brussels, and the place for which his testimony was destined, Paris, one cannot help wondering how much is really expressed in the testy allusion to a public which can listen without talking. By implication it claims a superiority for the Brussels theatre-goers ; but the words may also be intended to remind the French reader that the estimate formed of the music in Brussels was not to be gauged merely by the outward demonstration. One is led to believe some such thought ran in Gevaërt's mind, because Pigot speaks of the reception as " most favourable, but certainly not enthusiastic. The Bruxellois were too nearly related to the Parisians to understand completely a work so living and so frankly original at a first hearing." And, by way of confirmation, he quotes *Le Guide Musical* for the 10th of February, 1876, which, while declaring the music to be too personal and original for a public accustomed to well-worn formulae, recorded that its high merit was acknowledged by all.

In 1878 *Carmen* appeared at Marseilles, Lyons, Angers, Bordeaux, Leningrad, Naples, Florence, Ghent, Hanover, and Mainz ; altogether, a notable year in its history, a year whose record almost justifies Pigot's reference to the opera's triumphal journey over the world and to the acclamations of all civilized peoples. But, though the above-mentioned names indicate a sufficiently remarkable growth of interest, they do not tell the whole story of this period. The year in question witnessed the arrival of *Carmen* in English-speaking countries. The date of the first performance in London was the 22nd of June, 1878, the place Her Majesty's Theatre, and the governing hand that of Colonel Mapleson. On this occasion, the opera was sung in Italian under Sir Michael Costa, and Minnie Hauk, who had previously sung it at Brussels, took the part of Carmen. The success was one of the greatest ever experienced, having been eclipsed only by that of Gounod's *Faust*, given under the same management in 1863. In his *Memoirs* Mapleson relates some of the difficulties he had to encounter when the novelty was being prepared. Campanini did not take kindly to a tenor rôle that contained " no romance, and no love duet except with the *seconda donna*." Del Puente thought Escamillo's music must have been meant for one of the chorus ; Mlle. Valleria thought no better of Micaela's. By dint of strenuous exertion, the opera was put into rehearsal, when the singers became interested in their parts.

At the same theatre, on the 5th of February in the following year, the Carl Rosa Opera Company presented *Carmen* for the first time in English, the parts being thus distributed :

CARMEN	...	...	...	...	SELINA DOLARO
MICAELA	...	...	...	...	ELLA CROSMOND
FRASQUITA	...	...	...	...	JULIA GAYLORD
MERCEDES	...	...	...	...	JOSEPHINE YORKE
DON JOSÉ	...	...	...	...	DURWARD LELY
ESCAMILLO	...	...	...	...	WALTER BOLTON
DANCAIRO	...	...	...	...	AYNSLEY COOK
REMENDADO ...	...	...	...	CHARLES LYELL
CONDUCTOR	...	...	CARL ROSA		

And again at Her Majesty's, on the 8th of November, 1886, the opera was sung in London in French for the first time, with Galli-Marié in her original rôle.

There appears to be some doubt concerning the singer who first shouldered the part in the United States. Two names have been mentioned —those of Clara Louise Kellogg and Minnie Hauk. Most authorities award the palm to Mlle. Hauk. I am indebted to the late Mr. H. E. Krehbiel for the information that the first American performance of *Carmen* took place in the Academy of Music, New York, under the management of Colonel Mapleson, on the 23rd of October, 1878.[1] The principal singers were :

CARMEN	...	...	...	...	Mlle. HAUK
MICAELA	...	...	...	...	Mme. SINICO
DON JOSÉ	...	...	...	...	Sig. CAMPANINI
ESCAMILLO	...	...	...	...	Sig. DEL PUENTE
CONDUCTOR	...	...	Sig. ARDITI		

[1] It may not be without interest to state that, in the communication above referred to, Mr Krehbiel wrote : " Ten minutes ago I finished the first chapter of the English edition of Thayer's *Life of Beethoven* ".

113

In *The Complete Opera Book* Mr. Gustav Kobbé
remarks that America has had its *Carmen* periods,
and he informs us that the impression made by
Minnie Hauk remained potent until the appearance of Calvé. When Grau wished to fill his house,
he observes, all he had to do was to announce
Calvé as Carmen. She so dominated the character that it became impossible to revive the piece
at the Metropolitan Opera House until Geraldine
Farrar sang it in November, 1914. On this
occasion there was a remarkable cast, as Frances
Alda sang Micaela, Caruso Don José, and Pasquale
Amato Escamillo.

Since 1878, the popularity of Bizet's last work
has waxed to such an extent that it may be regarded as familiar, not only to the musicians but
to the musical public of all countries. There are
works which appeal to musicians, but do not
appeal to the public ; there are others which
appeal to the public, but do not appeal to musicians.
Carmen has admirers in both camps. There is,
however, another point of view, and it is neither
the musicians's nor the public's—that of the
interpretative artist. I think it may be affirmed
that the opera would not have passed through so
many hands if the music and the stage business
had not attracted singers, who evidently saw in
it great scope for the exploitation of their individual gifts. The Carmens have been many,
which is not surprising ; for Carmen is one of
those rôles that bring a reward to the talented

exponent, and can be convincingly interpreted in a hundred and one ways. To what extent the character of the gypsy has thrown its spell upon singers can be realised if the names of some of the best-known interpreters of it are mentioned : Marie Brema, Lucienne Bréval, Calvé, Chenal, Delna, Destinn, Farrar, Fremstad, Galli-Marié, Mary Garden, Maria Gay, Minnie Hauk, Marié de l'Isle, Kirkby Lunn, Georgette Leblanc Lilli Lehmann, Pauline Lucca, de Lussan, Marie Roze, Schumann-Heink, and Vix.

While these names call for no extended comment, it should be said that Marie Roze played the part of Carmen at least eight hundred times, and in English, French, and Italian. All the same, there exists a misconception which it would be well to dispel. It has been stated that Marie Roze was to have been the creator of Carmen. I had this direct from one source myself, and the same story will be found in the pages of Sutherland Edwards. He relates that she was not at first enamoured of the character, but, on being shown how much depended on the artist, consented to portray it. This she was prevented from carrying out by other important engagements. The same authority communicates the information that Bizet, impressed by Marie Roze's gifts, wrote *Carmen's* music specially for her, and that the allotting of the rôle to Galli-Marié, whose voice had a limited range, necessitated a re-writing of the same. The widow of the composer, Mme.

Bizet-Straus, authorises me to state that when writing the opera Bizet never thought of Marie Roze for the part. What she does state is that he had no particular singer in mind, or, rather that he thought of several singers when he started upon the score. It was only later, before finishing the work, that he decided for Galli-Marié.

Something ought to be said here of two other singers, Patti and Calvé, the former because in *Carmen* she made the one conspicuous failure of her career, the latter because she won world-wide fame in it. The full story of Patti as Carmen is excellently told by Mr. Herman Klein, to whose biography I cordially commend the reader.[1] Patti was at first evidently in love with the part. She said : " *J'aime tout ce qui est Carmen.* You will see me dance ; you will hear how I play the castanets." After reading these words, one thinks it strange that she did not score a success in the opera. Mr. Klein, however, offers an explanation ; " Her personality could express a vivacious nature with distinction and grace, but was never fitted for the embodiment of a commonplace woman of the people." Most of the music lay too low for her, and in 1885 she " had not developed her lower medium and chest tones to the degree of fullness that became noticeable in later years." She made changes in the music and introduced ornaments alien to the composer's design, a proceeding that was roundly condemned by the

[1] Herman Klein : *The Reign of Patti.*

press.   After the initial performance at Covent Garden, Patti appeared in the opera only once more there, which is scarcely astonishing when one hears from Mr. Klein, that, though Covent Garden was filled with a benevolent audience, the representation fell flat.   A later attempt with the part at the Metropolitan Opera House, New York, in 1887, was as unsuccessful, the audience being quite frigid.

There is no doubt that Calvé was temperamentally fitted to play Carmen, and it is surprising to read in her autobiography that it is not her favourite rôle.   While she likes the music, the character is antipathetic to her, as she finds in it only two redeeming qualities—truthfulness and courage. According to her own account, she struck out on a new line by wearing "the figured shawl, which is called in Spain the 'manton di Manilla', instead of the bolero and short skirt in which the part had always been costumed." In the dance she did not follow Galli-Marié, but indulged in "the true dance of the gitanas with its special use of the arms and the hands."[1]

Though Carmen is undoubtedly the centre and pivot of the opera, one should not forget the other chief personages, who have certainly not lacked distinguished representatives, as will be allowed if some of them are mentioned.   Micaela has been sung by Aïno Acté, Rose Delaunay,

[1] Emma Calvé : *My Life.*

Melba and Marie Thiéry ; Don José by Alvarez, Caruso, Jean de Reszké, Saléza, Tamagno, Van Dyck, and Zenatello ; Escamillo by Lassalle, Victor Maurel, Plançon, and Renaud. On the 11th of December, 1890, a special performance in aid of a monument to Bizet was given. On this occasion Galli-Marié (Carmen), Melba (Micaela), Jean de Reszké (Don José) and Lassalle (Escamillo) appeared. The receipts amounted to 42,000 francs.

With the passing of the years *Carmen* has won an honoured place in the repertoire of the companies which provide the British provinces with opera, and is, I suppose, at the present time a sure drawing-card. In the provincial towns the chief rôle has been associated mainly with Zélie de Lussan and Doris Woodall, but a history of Bizet's music in England would be bound to give prominence to the name of Sir Thomas Beecham. It is through him, at least, that English audiences of recent years have become acquainted with *La Jolie Fille de Perth*, given at Drury Lane in 1919, and *Les Pêcheurs de Perles* (in Italian) given at Covent Garden in 1920.

It will have been seen that the opera made headway in the world before Paris witnessed the act which Pierre Berton calls "the brilliant reparation." Georges Pioch talks ironically of the success "which quickly spread to the other countries of Europe, while France for eight years showed its originality by misunderstanding

Bizet."[1]   And then, commenting upon the difference between 1875 and 1883, he asks if one is to
believe that the Parisian public had lost its prud-
ishness or had gained in artistic clairvoyance.
If for eight years Paris stood aside and permitted
the opera to lead an emigrant's existence, it cannot be said that *Carmen* has since failed to establish
itself there.   I have ventured the opinion that it
needed but a touch to bring i. back to the Opéra
Comique, and the available figures reveal that the
1883 restoration was but the beginning of a
period of prosperity in Paris which lasts to this
very hour.   Thus, by the end of 1885 the work
had been given over 250 times ; by the end of
1895 the figures stood above 650 ; on the 23rd of
December, 1904, the thousandth performance
took place.   A census organised by a Paris
journal in 1911 resulted in 26,116 votes being
registered for *Carmen*, Massenet's *Manon* coming
second in the list with 20,524.

Two curious incidents connected with the
history of the opera will probably be remembered
by the reader.   Caruso sang the part of Don José
in San Francisco on the night of the great earth-
quake.   During the summer of 1907, Maria Gay
appeared in the opera along with Signor Zenatello
in South America.   So successful were those two
singers that at San Paulo an extra performance
was announced.   It was reported at the time that
about eight thousand people turned up at the box

[1] *Musica*, February 1905.

office, where they started to gather at four o'clock in the morning. In the evening, the crush was so great that several people were killed and many injured.

Few operas are without their inner history, and *Carmen* is no exception to the general rule. Most people will agree that the habanera, sung by Carmen just after her first appearance upon the stage, forms one of the freshest and most effective numbers in the entire work. It gives us a clue to the woman's nature ; it reveals her fickleness and makes us aware of her dangerous charm. Nothing, we say in listening to it, could better " strike her off," or provide a key to a character as complex as it is fascinating. The truth of the matter is that the habanera, which so often draws forth enthusiastic applause from the audience, was an afterthought. Had not Galli-Marié voiced her dissatisfaction with the piece which Bizet originally provided for her entrance, it would never have been heard. This original number, learnt and rehearsed, was in 6/8 time, and had, like its ultimate successor, choral support. The lady took exception to it on the grounds, apparently, of its tameness. It did not allow her scope for the employment of those arts and wiles which she felt should play their part at this particular juncture. She desired to make a great effect as she came on the stage ; she desired to make quite plain from the start what manner of person Carmen was. While the rehearsals progressed, she con-

fided in the composer. Time was running short ;
Galli-Marié was a person to be reckoned with, and
Bizet, having listened to the complaint, endeavoured to supply a piece in keeping with her re-
quirements. Whether the singer turned out to
be more than usually hard to please, or whether
Bizet was more than usually fastidious, I do not
pretend to know. The fact remains that he
wrote and re-wrote music for the entrance of
Carmen, and that the habanera we now have is
the thirteenth version. It is based upon a *chanson
havanaise*, which appears among the works of
Sebastian Yradier. Though now more or less
forgotten, this composer once enjoyed a considerable vogue. His *La Calesera* was sometimes sung
in the lesson scene of *The Barber of Seville* by Patti,
who included in her repertory also his *La Mantilla*.
It seems to be quite clear either that Bizet
based his piece upon the *chanson* in question, or
that he carried it very faithfully in his memory.
Gaudier, certainly, has no trouble in demon-
strating the close affinity which exists between
El Areglito, as it is called, and *L'amour est un
oiseau rebelle*. For one thing, the key of D minor
is common to both ; for another, the chromatic
design is equally common ; and the similarity
of the two refrains in the major is sufficiently
close to arrest the student. The adoption of the
theme by Bizet gave rise to some trouble that was
finally laid to rest by the insertion of the words,
" Imitated from a Spanish song, the property of

the editors of *Le Ménestrel*" on the first page of the habanera in the French score of the opera. In what I heard from one of his pupils, there may be some clue as to why Bizet thought of this Spanish melody. He visited the house of his pupil for the purpose of giving him lessons. The pupil's mother, who was born in South America, had a contralto voice for which Bizet expressed great admiration. She had studied with Madame Viardot, and at one time sang a great deal with Rossini. As can be well understood, she was fond of Spanish songs, one of which, contained in a music-book that held many Spanish manuscripts, she sang to Bizet very frequently. The habanera, my informant says, was inspired by this particular song.

There is something to be said also of three other excerpts ; the prelude to, the ensemble, *Quant au douanier*, and Micaela's song in, the third act. Of the first one might say, and there would be sense in the saying, that the little fragment had been projected into the score in order to provide contrast. It follows a vigorous and lively finale, and ushers in an act not lacking in incident and thrill. Bizet probably found it adequate for this purpose, but it will be observed that in its thematic material it bears no relationship to any other part of the opera. There is no Spanish touch in it, no echo, no reminiscence, no prophecy. When we have said that it is a pleasing page, well orchestrated and neatly rounded off, we have said all that can be said about it. Bizet intended at first to incorporate it in *L'Arlésienne*, for which the ensemble was likewise meant. Micaela's air, it will be remembered, found favour on the first night. Here, again, we look vainly for any Spanish characteristic, and we learn that this solo was originally destined for the *Grisélidis* which never reached completion. Sutherland Edwards affirms that two airs written for *Carmen*, one to be heard in the mountain scene, the other in the last act, have never been heard.

" Never prophesy unless you know," said that sound philosopher, Artemus Ward. Tschaikovsky, who was very fond of *Carmen*, did not hesitate to say what he thought of its future chances. Writing in 1880, he assumed the prophetic mantle and declared his conviction that in ten years Carmen would be the most popular opera in the world. If it is all but impossible to determine the work which occupies that fortunate position, there cannot be the slightest doubt that *Carmen* ranks among the most popular operas the world has ever heard.

CHAPTER III

Bizet's last meeting with Guiraud—Goes to Bougival—Illness and death—News causes sensation in Paris—Obsequies—Estimate of his career—His appearance—Method of work—Conversation and Recreations—Views on Music—A temperamental Man—Pianistic gifts—Astonishes Liszt—Work as teacher—Relationship with Musicians—His letters—A Critical Excursion—Unfinished works.

Not long after the production of *Carmen*, Bizet longed to shake the dust of Paris off his feet. The air of the city poisoned him. He had worked hard, had put the best of himself into *L'Arlésienne* and *Carmen*, had been compelled to wrestle with the innumerable difficulties inseparable from operatic production. Even while the rehearsals progressed, he found himself chasing the elusive goddess, Inspiration, in an endeavour to make Carmen's appearance all that the exponent wished it to be. When he left Paris he was not quite well, though his state of health, according to Ludovic Halévy, did not give rise to any apprehension. He had a little house at Bougival, a rustic spot of which he was extremely fond. Its tranquillity and beauty alike appealed to him after the rush and excitement of Paris. Here he could refresh his jaded spirit, and dream his idle dream by the side of the sleepy Seine. Marmontel speaks of " the charming villa at Bougival—a place he loved and where he often went in order to replenish his inspiration."[1]   What more natural than that, after the strain he had lately undergone, he should seek relaxation in a retreat so dear to his heart ?   Nature is a physician, which often heals the tired spirit, and restores to men harassed their lost buoyancy.

Bizet undoubtedly felt the call of fields, trees, and river.   His wife wished to postpone the date of departure from Paris until he was better able to stand the journey.   He would not hear of it. " I wish to go at once," was his cry.   On the eve of the journey, his " fidus Achates," Guiraud, went to see him in the evening after dinner.   At Bizet's request, he began to play upon the piano one or two parts of *Piccolino*, upon which he was then engaged.   Hardly had Guiraud touched the keys than Bizet told him that he could hear nothing, and took up another position, to the performer's left.   The voice which spoke was so weak that Guiraud, for an instant, was struck by it.   Guiraud played all that he had written ; Bizet listened attentively and made comments upon each piece.   From *Piccolino* the conversation drifted as conversations will, to all manner of topics.   Midnight came ; Guiraud made ready to leave.   He went down the steps and, looking up, saw Bizet, a candle in his hand, leaning towards him.   Some moments were spent in a final inter-

[1] A. Marmontel : *Symphonistes et Virtuoses.*

change of views, and the guest departed. That vision of Bizet, in his dressing-gown with the candle in his hand, was the last view Guiraud was destined to have of his friend. As late as the 2nd of June, Ludovic Halévy, who lived at the time at Saint Germain, visited Bizet, when he found him better.[1]

The first day at Bougival, says Pigot, passed well. Bizet took one of those walks he enjoyed so much, in company with his wife and Delaborde, the pianist. During the night he suffered much from oppression and suffocation. The doctor and Delaborde were called up. The doctor's report was reassuring ; he did not find the patient's condition dangerous. Bizet, still strong, required only rest. If a recurrence of the symptoms appeared, there was no need to seek medical advice. An attack even more alarming than the first came during the next night ; and, for a second time, the doctor and Delaborde were hastily summoned. The stricken man lay, as his wife thought, in peaceful sleep. . . .

Midnight sounded. At that very moment, the curtain rang down upon the thirty-third performance of *Carmen*. The young composer dead, the loving and distracted wife by his side, the undisturbed quiet of the countryside, the crowds issuing animatedly from the Opéra Comique—the imagination plays about the scene, touched as it is with sorrow and with tragedy.

[1] *Le Théâtre*, January 1905.

BIZET

" The mystery of the sad death of Bizet," says
Gaudier, "has not been completely elucidated.
One has spoken of embolism, and of oedema of the
glottis." On looking over Bizet's letters, one is
struck by the not infrequent allusions to his state
of health—allusions which may indicate much to
those who have a professional eye. As early as
January, 1858, he wrote to his mother that he was
well, except for an attack of cold worse than any
he had ever experienced at Paris ; he could not
get rid of it, and did not forget the homely cure
his mother recommended—a glass of hot milk
with nutmeg. A month later came a further
bulletin. His health in Rome was as poor as in
Paris, but his appetite grew. By March, he was
alarmed at loss of weight, which he could not
regain. At the end of the month, he reported a
sore throat that confined him to bed ; the enforced
laying up was rendered tolerable by the kindness
of his friends. Three days later and he voiced
the hope that he had not upset his people in Paris
—" an indisposition seen from a distance of four
hundred leagues becomes a grave illness." April
brought a lamentation that his trousers were
fifteen sizes too large, but he felt better after his
illness ; monotony of happiness and health
become tedious, and the fifteen days he had spent
in bed had done him good. From Naples, in
August of the following year, he sent off a letter
in which he mentioned a bad ulceration of the
throat that laid him up for eight days, and spoke

of the increasing inconvenience caused him by tonsilitis. In October he reported a return of his cold, accompanied by influenza and sore throat. But in the words he once wrote to his parents one finds a pathos lacking in the more prosaic details to which he usually confined himself. " I wish," he wrote, " for both of you perfect bodily health, without which there can be no spiritual health." [1]

Pigot reproduces a medical statement over the name of Dr. Lefevre. This tells us that Bizet was subject to frequent attacks of angina, which did not, however, seriously affect his health. The symptoms observed pointed to oedema of the glottis or to heart trouble as the cause of his death ; while a study of the case revealed that the composer had been for some years affected by the rheumatic diathesis. The biographer adds the evidence of Guiraud, who attributed Bizet's death to purulent resorption. From an early age Bizet suffered from attacks of angina of a mild character. These attacks returned periodically. Every year with the approach of Spring this weakness proclaimed itself, and he remained indoors. Then, the attack over, he went about as usual and recommenced his work. After his marriage he was free of this trouble for some years, but, unhappily, in March, 1875, a severe recurrence of the malady laid him low. Though he nursed himself assiduously, he was able to regain only a fair measure of the strength he had lost.

[1] Letter of the end of December, 1858.

Ludovic Halévy was seemingly one of the first to learn the sad news. He tells us that he was roused during the night of the 2nd–3rd of June at two o'clock. Mysteriously, as such advice will, a rumour that Bizet had just died circulated in Paris. Was it true ? Friends, admirers, and, no doubt, gossips, put the question to one another. At the Opéra Comique, if anywhere, they thought, the truth should be known. They, therefore, went to the Opéra Comique, which was soon besieged by people, both anxious and curious. In order to meet the needs of the situation, du Locle exhibited a telegram which Ludovic Halévy had dispatched to him early in the day, the 3rd of June. " The most horrible catastrophe," it read, " poor Bizet died last night. Ludovic Halévy " ; and Guiraud, only three days after that evening talk with his dearest friend, likewise received intimation of Bizet's death, by telegram from Bougival.

The funeral service took place on the 5th of June at the church of the Trinity, Paris. More than four thousand persons attended. Duchesne and Bouhy sang " Pie Jesu," adapted from *Les Pêcheurs de Perles*, the entire Pasdeloup orchestra played, among other things, the *Patrie* overture, and several artists from the Opéra Comique participated. Pasdeloup (to whom, by the way, *Carmen* is dedicated) was professionally engaged at Caen when he heard of Bizet's death. Without delay, he hurried to Paris in order to make the necessary arrangements. The pall-bearers were Gounod, Ambroise Thomas, Camille Doucet, and Camille du Locle ; and among the notabilities present were Ludovic Halévy, Massenet, Guiraud, Paladilhe, and Delaborde. At Père Lachaise, Jules Barbier, du Locle, and Gounod spoke in turn. Overcome by emotion, the last-named addressed only a few words to the gathering, but he repeated a confession that the young widow had made to him the day before : " There is not an hour, not a minute of the six years of happiness which my married life brought to me that I would not willingly live over again." At night, the Opéra Comique company assembled to play *Carmen*, and the artists, remarks Pigot, wept as they stepped upon the stage.

As might have been expected, the name of Bizet now assumed a new significance. At the opening of the *Concerts de l'Association Artistique*, Colonne devoted the second part of his programme to the memory of the recently deceased artist. In it a *lamento* specially composed by Massenet, a fragment of *L'Arlésienne* and the *Patrie* overture appeared ; and Galli-Marié delivered verses written by Louis Gallet. Further honours were to be paid to Bizet with the passing of time. At the hundredth performance of *Carmen* the bust in marble by Paul Dubois was installed in the foyer of the Opéra Comique. It represents Bizet as he was in the last year of his life. I am informed by one who was intimately associated with him,

that this bust is a masterpiece of verisimilitude,
and, to my unskilled eye, it seems an excellent
piece of work. A bronze cast of it is to be found
at Père Lachaise. In response to many requests,
the municipal council of Paris decided to per-
petuate the composer's memory by naming after
him a street at Passy. On the 2nd of June, 1912,
a tablet was placed upon the house at Bougival in
which he died. Mlle. Madeleine Roche read
two sonnets, *La Maison de Bizet* and *Pour Georges
Bizet*, expressly written by André Rivoire and
Lucie Delarue-Mardrus, respectively. Representatives of the state and of music assembled to
pay homage to one of France's most gifted
musicians, and Xavier Leroux, at that time vice-
president of the Society of Authors, delivered an
oration.

The last phase holds us in thrall. We are
aware of the strong fascination which it exercises ;
we turn again, and yet again, to a study of it ; we
examine it in all its bearings ; we ask ourselves
questions that can never be satisfactorily answered.
At the close of a long life, Haydn declared that he
had just begun to understand the wind instruments. Towards the end, Beethoven felt as
though he had penned but a few notes. Just
before his death, Schubert arranged to take lessons
in counterpoint with the learned Sechter. The
romantic Weber, riddled by tuberculosis, sang
his swan song in *Oberon*. His battle over,
Wagner, the magnificent fighter, breathed the

accents of renunciation in *Parsifal*. Tschaikov-sky made his exit with a *Symphonie Pathétique*, in which he gathered up all the tears of an emotional and excitable world. Verdi, probably most re-markable of all, bade us adieu with a graceful smile, and offered those who lamented his lack of science a rollicking fugue.

From this peculiar, this all but inescapable, spell of what may be called the last hour, the writers who have treated the subject of these modest pages have not been immune. In fact, most of the commentators who have taken up their pens to write of Bizet enlarge on the loss which French music suffered by his early death. One would be less than human did not one feel an acute pang of regret in reading of it ; and the feeling is intensified by the fact that he died exactly three months after the first performance of what is universally acknowledged to be his finest achievement. The sense of something lost, of something denied us by a sinister fate, takes possession of us. We think of *Carmen*, and, in the thinking, invade the treacherous realms of speculation. We say to ourselves that we have been defrauded ; that we ought to have had its successors, which we vaguely see crowned with the same meritorious qualities. Bizet died in the thirty-seventh year of his age ; had he attained the three score years and ten of the Psalmist, he would surely have added greatly to the glory of French music. Thus we talk. In other words, our distress and sorrow at his early death carry us into the region of sentiment.

One is not hard-hearted when one says that this sort of speculation is both idle and foolish. A person who knew only the works which preceded *Carmen* could not have foretold it ; a person knowing *Carmen* cannot possibly form any reliable conception of its possible, or probable, successors. When people say that French music lost much by Bizet's death, they are simply throwing History out of the window. Some composers, like Bizet, have died young ; Purcell, Mozart, Schubert, Bellini, and Chopin, are of their number. Others, like Handel, Wagner, Liszt, Verdi, and Saint-Saëns, have lived to a good old age. It is easy, and perhaps natural, for us to suggest to ourselves that those who lived long said all they had to say, and that those who were cut off early died with some of, if not all, their music in them. In his *Musicians of To-day* Romain Rolland laments the passing of Bizet. " What a place Bizet might have taken in our art," he says, " if he had lived only twenty years longer ! " M. Croche, alias Debussy, similarly observes that " Bizet died too soon." Can one be so sure of this ? For myself, I feel that neither I, nor anyone else, can tell. In an article on Rossini's *Stabat Mater*, Wagner affirms that nothing has been heard of that master for ten years, since " he sat in Bologna, ate pastry, and made wills." I am not disposed to credit many other composers

with such a fantastic way of filling their time ; but
I am disposed to say that dates and years are remarkably deceptive. Has Mascagni ever
" topped " the sensational success he won in 1890
with *Cavalleria Rusticana* ; what would some of
the critics have said if Mascagni had died after
his extraordinary entrance into the world of
opera ?   Does Max Bruch mean very much more
than his violin concerto in G minor ?   Humper-
dinck died in 1921 without excelling *Hänsel and
Gretel*, which was produced in 1893.   Hamish
MacCunn seems destined to be known only by his
overture, *Land of the Mountain and the Flood*.
Goldmark lived till 1915, without adding to the
prestige he won with *The Queen of Sheba*, which
belongs to 1875, and the *Rustic Wedding* symphony, which belongs to 1887.   And who could
have foretold the future, and almost unique,
career of Boïto from the enthusiastic reception
accorded to his *Mefistofele*, when it was presented
in revised form at Bologna in 1875 ?

Bizet might have contributed generously and
nobly to the music of his time ;   beyond this I
cannot go.   He was a musician and found his
happiness in producing music ;   I cannot see him
living for long without his pen in hand.   There is,
I repeat, not a shred of evidence to show that, had
he lived to the age of eighty, he would not have
written his *Falstaff*.   By that I mean that there is
not a shred of evidence to show that he would
have ceased writing ;   I mean that the expression

of his thoughts was second nature to him ; and I mean, more particularly, that the *Carmen* experience would not have caused him to call a halt. But the production of music is one thing ; the production of music of outstanding merit, another. For all we know, *Carmen* might have been his *Queen of Sheba*, his *Land of the Mountain and the Flood* ; it might have been the one fine flowering of his spirit. The spectacle of a man putting himself into a work in a way he never managed to do subsequently is not unknown to art. Again, for all we know, *Carmen* might have been the forerunner of many operas, whose beauties we cannot even guess. I admire and enjoy the work, but I should be lacking in candour if I said that I could honestly add my voice to those who confidently proclaim that French music lost much by Bizet's early death. In saying this, I cast no slur upon his reputation ; I detract not a whit from his remarkable abilities. The gestation and realisation of musical works is an art at once subtle and mysterious ; man is a delicate and finely-tempered machine, easily put out of commission. One hesitates to dogmatise about the unknowable.

A study, however absorbing, of the last few months of Bizet's life ought not to engage attention to the exclusion of a wider one, that of his career. How should one describe that career ? Was it a failure or a success ; or was it one of those careers, more difficult to describe, that lean now to one side, now to the other, of the border-

line ? Before we can make any progress, it is
imperative to settle what the words failure and
success represent. There are failures that, para-
doxically, are successes ; successes that, as para-
doxically, are failures. The name we use is
always settled by the standpoint which we take
up, by the test to which we submit works of art.
According to the higher, the ethical view, work
well and truly done is always successful ; for the
ethical view takes no account of reward. The
very doing of the task, be it worth doing, is itself
the worker's recompense. The ethical view
teaches that to deserve success is already to grasp
it. What the world has to say, what the world is
prepared to pay, does not affect the estimate. A
work of art is not made any greater because one
thousand people enjoy it to-day, while only one
hundred enjoyed it yesterday. If the popular
view were an index of the value of a work, we
should be compelled to see in *The Bohemian Girl*
and *Maritana* two of the masterpieces of music ;
which, as Euclid says, is absurd. Popularity has
its own meaning and its own lesson ; but it
neither means nor teaches anything unless the
source of it be carefully examined. At the first
plebiscite, the vote went to Barabbas.

There is another view ; the everyday or, if you
will, the mundane view. A large number of
people are always anxious to know if this man, or
the other, won the ear of the crowd, if he stood
well with those in authority, if his following were

large, his sales big, his influence wide. Bizet's career was curious, and in some respects almost unique. He did not create a work which sent Paris into a veritable delirium of ecstasy; he did not taste the sweets of blinding triumph which Liszt knew; he did not enjoy an enormous vogue, comparable to that of Massenet. His fame increased after his death; his status is, perhaps, higher to-day than it was at any time during his life. This said, we must hold the scales very delicately. The acknowledgment of what he did not enjoy need not send us to the other extreme. Many economic circumstances separate what is commonly called success from utter neglect. A man to whom the triumph of triumphs is denied is not necessarily a man left upon the doorstep to beg a crust. It is when we endeavour conscientiously to form an estimate of Bizet's career that its peculiarity is seen in a white light.

Perhaps the truth lies somewhere between the opinion of the eulogistic Pigot, and that of the epigrammatical and downright Gauthier-Villars. Be this as it may, we cannot blind ourselves to several facts that stare us in the face. Bizet was never called upon to suffer that spiritual isolation which so many artists have known; he was never forlorn. His parents guarded and guided him in the tender years of infancy and boyhood. During his pupilage, his masters looked upon him with a kindly eye, and did everything in their power to help his onward march. He won the coveted *prix de Rome.* Writing to Paul Lacombe in 1866, he refers to the lessons, the heavy work for several editors, and the other affairs which devour his life.[1] Practically from the date of his return to Paris, he was importuned by theatrical managers. If the public was at best coldly courteous, if the critics sometimes steeped their pens in vinegar, those influential gentlemen, who held the keys of the operatic heaven, neither forgot his existence, nor left him severely alone.

All this is made abundantly plain in an admirably succinct article by Emile Vuillermoz,[2] who declares that Bizet's career " was not tragic, not even sad." The writer reminds us that he never wrote except to order ; that the directors of the theatres brought their libretti to him ; that, the last bar of his works written, they went straight away into rehearsal. He goes on to say that Bizet never knew violent checks ; that his operas generally won success at the rehearsals, though they did not sufficiently attract the crowd in order to furnish a fruitful career. He was quite young when the Opéra Comique commissioned *Le Guzla de l'Emir,* and Carvalho commissioned *Les Pêcheurs de Perles* for the Théatre-Lyrique. *Ivan le Terrible* was composed for the last-named stage, then came *La Jolie Fille de Perth.* He was asked to finish *Noë.* Louis Gallet took the libretto of *Djamileh* from Duprato in order to give it to Bizet;

[1] First letter to Lacombe.
[2] *Musica,* June 1912.

and du Locle mounted it without hesitation. Carvalho ordered *L'Arlésienne*, part of which Pasdeloup introduced to the concert-room. The Opéra Comique commissioned *Carmen*, and, a week later, apparently entered into negotiations with Bizet, Meilhac and Halévy for a new work. In addition to all this, there was talk of Bizet's writing *Le Cid* at the instigation of the singer, Faure, a score which was to have been played at the Opéra. Reviewing these facts, I imagine that few composers would be tempted to write down such a career as an unsuccessful one. But in order to complete the picture, it should be said that Bizet had friends whose belief in him, and whose loyalty towards him, have never been called in question. His married life was successful and happy. " Esteemed highly, officially considered a master," says Vuillermoz, " Bizet therefore knew all through his life the most flattering attentions and had not to fight like the majority of composers." What, of course, impresses us as more than a trifle curious, is that though, during his life, he never scored one of those overwhelming victories that go down to history as an event to be remembered, the theatrical managers did not keep him at arm's length. This alone speaks of a confidence in his musical powers. The managers were evidently persuaded that he had it in him to gain such a success, and they hoped to draw the winning number out of the lucky bag.

What are we to say, then, of Bizet's career ?

If it be contended that he had to tolerate some ill-natured or ill-informed criticism, he was not in this different from the majority of his brethren. If he had enemies, we may well ask what man of personality has ever been without them. If he had his trials and tribulations, we say simply that the path trodden by artists is never entirely free of them. If he had his moments of despondency, are they not known to all sensitive and temperamental individuals ? So far as I can discover, there is nothing in Bizet's career to render it more tragic than that of most composers. It was, in fact, much more successful, much less tragic, than those of many. I surmise that he was not what would now be considered a rich man ; but I should be surprised to learn that he ever found himself in the desperate straits that Wagner more than once knew. He was not so obscure as Schubert ; he was not tied to a Xanthippe like Haydn ; he was not assailed by the arch-fiend which attacked Beethoven and Smetana. In his volume, *Mes Souvenirs*, Massenet observes that " life had been very hard for him." I do not know whether Massenet's judgment was arrived at by comparing Bizet's career with his own, or whether, in using the words, he thought of the sensitiveness of the man. To me it seems an extreme statement. Remembering his vocation, remembering that tastes and views differ, that the doors of theatres do not always open to the touch, that the world is a large debating society wherein the acrimonious voice may always be heard, I cannot but believe that Bizet had much for which to be grateful.

The classics, says Busoni somewhere, have been killed with respect. In like manner, composers have often suffered at the hands of those who place above their heads unbecoming halos. Many people see in the men whose works they admire impossibly impeccable figures, such as exist only in the remote world of extravagant romance. If we realise that composers, after all, are only human, we lose something ; but the something which we lose is unreal, whereas what we gain is of definite value. To claim too much for your man is to put yourself wrong with History, and, incidentally, to do your man an injustice ; for, even posthumously, men have to live up to their reputations. Far be it from me to present Bizet either as a god or as an angel. He was a man who moved among men, a man who breathed the air of his time.

In appearance he was interesting, though not remarkably striking. His confidence and energy were stamped upon his features. In looking at the bust by Paul Dubois, we behold a visage that betokens mental alertness. A shock of curly hair wreathes the brow, the nose is sensitive, the mouth seems ready to smile, a fair beard covers the chin. The only thing the bust does not tell us is, perhaps, that the composer was very short-sighted.

141

"As a child," says Marmontel, "Bizet was fair and fresh-coloured, full-faced, but very alert. As a young man his features became firmer. His clear look, his open countenance, his smiling mouth, indicated a character of no little energy. His dominant expression was one of confidence."

"Under an exterior somewhat severe," writes Imbert, "he hid a heart of gold. For him, friendship was no vain word."

When he came to attack a work, he made considerable progress with it before he committed any part to paper. Here is a description of his method which I have received from an excellent source :

"He conceived all his works in his mind without writing down anything, except occasionally, but very exceptionally, some bars that he noted in a pocket book. I have heard him play *L'Arlésienne* and *Carmen* in their entirety before he had written a line. It was the same with *Le Cid*, the book of which had been entrusted to him, and of which he had entirely composed three acts that he had not time to write down ; so the book passed subsequently into the hands of Massenet."

Bizet worked by preference during the evening and through the night, often till the grey hours of dawn ; when particularly wrapt up in his task, he laboured at it unceasingly.

His conversation was simple and of a good humour ; he loathed obscurity, but not infrequently indulged in paradox. Nothing gave him more enjoyment than to take a walk in the country during the summer. He rarely went to the opera, and then only to hear a new work or an interesting artist. In his lighter moments, when he threw off the cares of the day, he would parody the airs of Méhul and Boieldieu, by embellishing them and introducing obsolete ornaments.[1] He was sensitive to criticism, though he did not always betray the fact.   His frank and honest nature, according to Marmontel, suffered cruelly from the often excessive harshness of the critics.[2]

> " Ah ! believe me," he wrote in 1867, " biassed criticism is a cruel, terrible, and mortal weapon." [3]

And again:

> " I have a hatred of pedantry and of false erudition.   Certain critics of the third or fourth rank use and abuse a *soi-disant* technical jargon, as unintelligible to themselves as to the public." [4]

In a letter of 1869 to Paul Lacombe, he said apropos of a sonata his pupil had written :

> " There are few critics competent to hear, and fewer still to read a sonata."

But if he took to heart what the critics said, he was not carried away by an exaggerated idea of his own importance.   Even when at Rome, at the period, that is to say, when so many clever young men suffer from swelled head, he wound up a passage characteristically direct, very sanguine, and youthful in its manner, with the words :

[1] Marmontel.
[2] *Ibid.*
[3] Pigot.
[4] *Ibid.*

" . . . . but you know I am not a fool, you understand what I wish to say. Remember that *en loge* I was never deceived as to the relative merits of my cantatas."[1]

Seven years later, he wrote his first letter to Lacombe, who had inquired about lessons. After a few preliminary words, he starts off :

"I am twenty-eight years old. My musical baggage is small enough."

He proceeds to give an account of his achievements—an opera, very much discussed, attacked and defended, some songs, seven or eight piano pieces, symphonic fragments, and a new important work to be given in a few months. Something of the same attitude of mind is discernible in the letter that he wrote to Weber, critic of the Paris newspaper *Le Temps*, when *La Jolie Fille de Perth* came out. Weber had taken exception to the copious roulades allotted to Catherine in that opera. Bizet, reading his notice, felt impelled to write to Weber, not to justify himself, or to complain, but to tell him that he, too, in his heart renounced the "false gods." He had made concessions which he regretted. The school of tol-de-rol, roulades, and shams, was dead, and to be interred without tears, regrets, or emotion.

The most prominent reference of a financial nature to be found in his letters is that which occurs in a communication to his parents written towards the end of December, 1858 ; therein he

[1] Letter to his mother of the 19th March 1859.

144

discloses a plan. When he has one hundred thousand francs neither his father nor he will give lessons ; they will live the life of independent gentlemen. One hundred thousand francs is nothing—two little successes at the Opéra Comique. A success like *Le Prophète* brings in almost a million. In a letter from Rome, dated the 11th of March, 1858, he relates how his monthly pension of two hundred francs is spent ; one hundred and sixty-five on food, attendance, piano, laundry, gloves, stamps, and so on, leaving thirty-five for cigars, tips, and the like. He does not complain of the allowance. When replying to Lacombe in the letter just referred to, he is compelled to say something about his fees. After protesting his distaste for the subject, he states that, with so much to do, he has to charge, not for his advice, but for the time occupied by the lessons. His fee is twenty francs per lesson ; on an average, his time is worth fifteen francs an hour.

Bizet early showed his preferences among the composers, and Marmontel encouraged his pupil to unburden himself. As we trace his likes and dislikes down the years, we come to the conclusion that he was extremely eclectic ; that he enjoyed music of very many styles ; that his impulsiveness often carried him away. He had never, perhaps, during his short and busy life, retired to an ivory tower in order to think out things dispassionately ; he had not quietly and calmly

BIZET

worked his way to some kind of definite aesthetic creed, by virtue of which one can alone gain a true critical perspective. To ask such of a composer is, perchance, to ask too much. The creative mind, and particularly the creative mind of the spontaneous order, is not often akin to the critical one.

The ease with which Bizet passed from one work to another, like a bee gathering honey in its flight from flower to flower, has not been neglected by Gauthier-Villars. "Gounod, Halévy and Marmontel were the only guides of the young pilgrim on the paths of Art," he remarks, and thereafter he speaks of the indulgence exhibited by the author of *Carmen* towards all the music which met his gaze. In the passage indicated, the critic quotes some of the confessions which fell from Bizet's lips :

"I love Italian music." "I am German by conviction, in heart and soul." "Rome is the true home of artists."

Others have, less sarcastically, given us some light on Bizet's preferences.

He considered Stephen Heller one of the best of modern composers[1] ; he recognised the greatness of some of Wagner's conceptions ; he admired the dramatic power of Verdi. His predilection for Italian and German music did not blind him to the beauties of the home-made article. Gounod and Ambroise Thomas were

[1] Galabert.

146

sources of enjoyment. He professed a great
regard for Thomas's *Hamlet,* and arranged it for
piano, both for two and four hands.[1]   As a young
man, he preferred Mozart to Beethoven, and
Rossini to Meyerbeer.[2]   On the 8th of October,
1858, he is more than ever convinced that Mozart
and Rossini are the two great masters :

> "While admiring with all my power Beethoven and Mey-
> erbeer, I feel that my nature draws me more to the art that
> is pure and facile, than to dramatic passion.   So is it with
> painting, Raphael is the same man as Mozart ; Meyerbeer
> feels as Michael Angelo felt. . . . I have come to recognise
> in Verdi, a man of genius, pursuing the most deplorable path
> that ever was."

In an undated letter inscribed to Mme. Halévy,
he contrasts Auber and Berlioz :

> "Auber, who had much talent, and few ideas, was almost
> always understood, while Berlioz, who had genius without
> talent, was almost never understood ! "[3]

Comments on Gounod's art appear frequently.
Writing from Rome on the 27th of January, 1858,
he rejoices in the success of *Le Médécin malgré lui.*
On the 8th of February, 1858, he declares Gounod
to be perhaps the only composer able to give useful
advice to a singer.   On the 16th of May, 1858, he
reverts to Gounod's latest piece ; after looking
over the score, he finds it the best thing done in

[1] Marmontel.
[2] Imbert.
[3] Ganderax.

the *opéra-comique genre* since Grétry, including Grisar. In the 31st of December, 1858, he enlarges upon Gounod's sympathetic nature:

> " How one willingly submits to this warm imagination ! . . . he is the only man among our modern musicians who truly loves his art."

The enthusiasm reaches its height evidently about 1859–1860. On the 19th of February, 1859, at any rate, he tells his mother that " Gounod is a composer, essentially original, and in imitating him, one remains a pupil." On the 9th of December, 1859, Gounod is " the best equipped of the French composers." On the 23rd of June, 1860, " Gounod alone is master ; after him, there is nobody "—which is certainly very high praise.

By the 11th of March, 1867, when he writes to Paul Lacombe, he is able to declare that the choral symphony is for him the culminating point " of our art " ; and later, on the 29th of May, 1871, writing to Mme. Halévy, he calls it " the greatest page of our art." As for Verdi, of whom something has been said, he affirms, in a letter of the 19th February, 1859, that the Italian is a man of undoubted talent, who lacks the essential quality which goes to make great masters—style. The following year he echoes a current rumour that Verdi will write no more, adding that if the master did, it was to be doubted whether he would repeat such flashes of genius as may be found in *Il Trovatore*, *La Traviata*, and the fourth act of

Rigoletto—a false prophecy, as it proved. He found *Don Carlos* pretentious. In it Verdi was no longer Italian ; he wished to write like Wagner.[1] Chopin was for him the only man who knew how to compose music that seemed to be improvised. In the Pole he discerned " a charming, strange, and inimitable personality." [2] Pigot and Galabert testify to his Bach enthusiasm. " All his life," says the former, " he remained a fervent and passionate disciple of Bach." What he wrote to Paul Lacombe on the 11th of March, 1867 is as near to an *apologia pro vita sua* as he came. In this letter he announces his eclecticism. He thrills when he hears Italian music, so facile, indolent, amorous, and passionate. He delivers the aforementioned pronouncement that he is German by conviction, in heart and soul. He quotes excerpts from *Norma*, *I Puritani*, *La Sonnambula*, *Rigoletto*, *Il Trovatore*, *La Traviata*, and *Don Pasquale* ; leave him these, and you could do what you liked with the rest. Beethoven he places at the head of all the symphonists ; he is worthy to be ranked with Dante, Michael Angelo, Shakespeare, Homer, Moses. Neither Mozart, with his divine form, nor Weber, with his power and originality, nor Meyerbeer, with his dramatic gift, is able to dispute the palm with the Titan, the Prometheus of music. Of the important Wagner question, there remains, of course, some-

[1] Imbert.
[2] *Ibid.*

thing to be said. It can most conveniently be treated when I deal with Bizet's music from a critical standpoint.

Gaudier very skilfully contributes to our knowledge of Bizet's likes and dislikes in his interesting chapter on the composer's musical evolution. Here the reader can quickly learn much that will be invaluable to him. Gaudier remarks Bizet's curious grouping of Beethoven and Meyerbeer, and his equally curious grouping of Meyerbeer and Michael Angelo. Very wisely, the commentator reminds us that the Meyerbeer-Michael Angelo association was established at a time when the composer of *Les Huguenots* passed for a thinker and a great master of the emotions. Some of the old musicians meant nothing to Bizet. Boieldieu and Nicolo did not exist ; *La Dame Blanche* roused his ire ; Haydn and Grétry put him to sleep.

Such contradictions, waverings, changes of taste and revised estimates, as are met with, take firm hold of the student of Bizet's life. He had found his path, he was an *opéra-comique* man, yet he nursed symphonic ambitions, and thought of making a début at the Grand Opera with *Le Cid*. He wrote a *Te Deum*, contemplated an oratorio, and announced himself more pagan than Christian. He set his heart on *Roma*, and, when Saint-Saëns said to him : " As they do not want us in the theatre, let us take refuge in the concert-hall," he replied : " It is easy for you to speak.

I'm not made for the symphony. The theatre is necessary for me ; I can do nothing without it."
He was German in heart and soul ; he loved the facile music, the spontaneous melody of the South, with its expansiveness, its easy charm, its amorous accents ; nor could he forget that he was French. Rome was the true habitat of the artist, Germany the country of music. He was reproached with too much science, and disdained *kapellmeister* music. He was charged with Wagnerism, and Nietzsche found in him the antithesis of Wagner, the man who could mediterraneanise music, infuse it with a southern warmth, and rescue it from the inhospitable north. He was a pianist of enormous ability, who never played in concert, and composed very little for the instrument of which he was so consummate a master. It is not only *la donna* who is *mobile*.

All this may seem exceedingly disconcerting, and far from encouraging for those who, having read his confessions, still seek the true Bizet. The true Bizet, forsooth, lies in the confessions themselves, and in the picture to which they all contribute. What they tell us is, in reality, easily apprehended. We see that the man was impulsive, we see that his impulsiveness was of the kind which often accompanies the artistic nature. It was born of ardour, of enthusiasm, of emotion ; it fretted at philosophic restraint, and liked none too well the caution and hesitancy native to the cooler mind. When we have learned

this, we have learned also that some of the contradictions are, to speak exactly, seeming ones.
He had his prejudices and his limitations, which is
a way of saying that he was a man, and not an
angel or a god.   There is nothing to show that,
when he delivered himself on a composer or a
work, he was not sincere.   The words were the
expression of his thought.   Unless I am much in
error, frankness was habitual with him.   He had
little liking, and less gift, for the niceties of diplo-
matic phraseology.   He would not, I think, have
made a successful courtier.   It is because I read
his personality in this way that I claim authenticity
for his many utterances, and recommend that they
be laid under tribute.   Man changes impercep-
tibly with the passing of the years ; he changes
spiritually, as well as physically.   The man of
fifty is not likely to read and reread the books that
brightened his school-days ; if he does, he can
hardly hope to experience the early thrill.   Literary
critics observe that the poetry of old age differs
essentially from the poetry of full-blooded youth.

> " . . . . . . I have learned
> To look on nature, not as in the hour
> Of thoughtless youth ; but hearing oftentimes
> The still, sad music of humanity,"

writes Wordsworth.   But if a change be a condition of all life, it is apt to be greater and more
frequent in the case of the finely-strung individual
than in that of the phlegmatic one.   Bizet, as we

see, changed, and changed with the frequency of
the temperamental man. It is hardly necessary
to say, therefore, that the Bizet of this moment
was not the Bizet of that ; there were a hundred
Bizets, each of them a true one. This makes it
plain that his opinions are valuable more for the
light they throw upon his own personality than
for any contribution to our knowledge of the men
and works with whom and which they are concerned.

As I have recorded, he never appeared in public
as a pianist, notwithstanding his ability at the
keyboard. This is the more astonishing as he
was not merely an efficient player, but a really
remarkable one, to whose prowess every person
who heard him bears the most eloquent witness.
Writing in *Les Debats* in October, 1863, Berlioz
speaks of him as an " incomparable score reader."

> " His pianistic talent," he continues, " is moreover so great
> that in the renderings of orchestral works which he gives at
> sight, no technical difficulty is able to embarrass him. Since
> Liszt and Mendelssohn, such a remarkable reader has never
> been seen."

" Père Marmontel," as he was called at the Conservatoire, says :

> " In becoming a composer and one of the most gifted masters
> of dramatic and symphonic art, Bizet remained a virtuoso,
> an intrepid reader, and a model accompanist. His execution,
> always bold and brilliant, acquired a remarkable sonorousness,
> a variety of timbres and nuances, which gave to his playing an

inimitable charm when he interpreted his orchestral trans-
scriptions, and above all, his vocal pieces *L'Ecole du chanteur
italien, allemand et français.*"

Little wonder was it that he astounded the
group of hearers in Rome. Galabert allows him
talent of the first order, and informs us that Bize.
considered a composer ought to become a pianist
in order to gain precision in the matter of form.
By way of proof, he quoted to Galabert the great
composers who had been fine pianists—Bach,
Mozart, Beethoven, and Meyerbeer. The careful execution of Bach's fugues appeared to him to
be indispensable for the making of a good musician. After having heard Delaborde play the
pedal piano at Erard's, he thought of writing
piano music.

Mention of the pianist calls to mind a story
that Pigot relates. As I heard it from one well
qualified to know, it would appear to be authentic,
though Isadore Philipp, in an article presently to
be referred to, does not assume responsibility.
It is a story which makes one realise how enormously gifted Bizet was as reader and executant ;
it is a story which, for the thousandth time, lays
bare the large-heartedness of Liszt. One evening
in 1861, Halévy gave a dinner party at which
several friends were present, among them, Liszt
and the young Bizet. After dinner, the guests
made their way to Halévy's study. Some time
passed in conversation, then Liszt sat down at the
piano. He played one of his latest pieces, at the

period quite unknown, full of the pitfalls and extra-ordinary difficulties which characterise so much of his music. He tossed off the piece gloriously, and was surrounded by the enchanted hearers, who complimented him in flattering terms. " Yes," he is reported to have said, " the piece is difficult, horribly difficult, and I know only two pianists in Europe capable of playing it as it is written and at the proper *tempo*, Hans von Bülow and myself." Halévy, who was beside the piano, drew Bizet's attention to a remarkable passage in the piece Liszt had just made known to them ; this he indicated by playing a few notes. Turning to the keyboard, Bizet repeated the passage in question without hesitation. Liszt and Halévy were com-pletely dumbfounded. " Wait, my young fellow, wait," exclaimed Liszt, " I have the manuscript here ; it will help your memory." The manu-script was set upon the piano. To the surprise of those gathered together, Bizet began to play the piece with boldness and confidence, and pro-ceeded triumphantly to the last bar. The com-pany gave him an ovation. Halévy smiled the smile of satisfaction at the success gained by his pupil. Liszt held out his hand to the intrepid virtuoso. " My dear friend," he said, " I believed there were only two men able to grapple success-fully with the difficulties I have introduced into this piece ; I was wrong ; we are three, and, in justice, I ought to add that the youngest of the three is perhaps the most audacious and most brilliant."

A contribution on the subject of Bizet as a pianist is to be found in the article by Isadore Philipp previously mentioned.[1] He emphasises Bizet's sense of the pedal, which impressed Paul Lacombe also, and finds in the collection *Le Pianiste Chanteur* proof of cunning in the making of arrangements. Being himself a pianist and pedagogue, it must have struck Philipp as curious that so gifted a player did not more often write for the piano. He touches upon the pieces that exist ; the little fragments *à la* Schumann,[2] six agreeable *Songs without words à la* Mendelssohn, the *Variations Chromatiques*, a pale imitation of Schumann's *Études Symphoniques*, and *La Chasse Fantastique à la* Stephen Heller. In these pages Philipp looks in vain for originality.

The man felt that he lacked something which a real composer of piano music must have. To Lacombe, assuredly, he confessed how difficult it was to write for the instrument, though he once coquetted with the idea of producing a piano concerto. It is certain that he did not put the very best of himself into his piano music. It does not contain his finest thought. The piano, from which he drew such poetry, was a secondary medium. He knew its secrets, its idiosyncrasies, its capabilities and limitations, but never, somehow, caught the magic when he settled down to

[1] *Musica*, June 1912.
[2] Bizet, it will be remembered, transcribed Schumann's Studies for pedal piano (op. 56) for piano duet.

augment its literature. Of his prowess, there is no diversity of opinion. Emile Perrin, speaking on the 10th of June, 1876, at the inauguration of the monument at Père Lachaise, voiced the feelings of the musical world when he called him " an incomparable executant " ; and Saint-Saëns was sure that, if he had wished, he might have acquired great renown as a virtuoso. What caused the composer of *Carmen* to shrink from the platform was a fear that he should be classed as a pianist, and that his reputation as a creative artist should suffer at the hands of a public suspicious of versatility. A caricaturist once depicted Thalberg with ten fingers on each hand. Had the man with the pencil heard Bizet, he would have been sorely tempted to repeat his anatomical inexactitude.

It will have been gathered that teaching absorbed some of Bizet's time. From the published letters addressed to Lacombe, of which I have so often spoken, one obtains the best glimpse of him as an instructor. He had a healthy dislike of false erudition, of pedagogic word-spinning, of the superfluities and perplexities with which some professors invest their subjects in order to lend them an air of profundity. He did not exhibit much patience with those who turn music into a dull game to be played on five lines and four spaces, according to rules from which there is no appeal, or approach it as the deepest of esoteric mysteries. He liked a statement clear and concise ; he liked to deal with the essentials, and with them alone ; he pursued simplicity and shunned the dryly academic, as though it were the very devil himself. I am much deceived if his aim were not to make the acquisition of a technique as easy a matter as possible. The Lacombe letters make this quite plain. In the first of them, he says that composition is difficult to deal with by correspondence ; it is necessary to see, hear, discuss, and know, in order to work profitably. Counterpoint, fugue, and orchestration, on the other hand, are able to be dealt with successfully by this means "I have tried it," he writes. It has been asserted, and not unreasonably, that in this series of letters Bizet shows a complacency of which teachers are seldom guilty. Taking the examples of work that Lacombe sent him, he quickly spots reminiscences and echoes. "You know the masters, notably Mendelssohn, Schumann, and Chopin, whom you seem to cherish with a tenderness somewhat exclusive," runs one comment. Again, "You certainly like Schumann"; again, he talks of "this little Verdian excursion"; and yet again, pounces upon passages which recall the *Kreutzer* sonata and the first concerto of Chopin.

But the general tone of the letters is most certainly one of encouragement. Few teachers would be disposed to praise as highly as he does the passages which evidently deserved praise, nor would many of them be content to place them-

selves on so modest a platform. For Bizet, the
teacher, it should be said, did not look down upon
struggling fledglings from an Olympian height of
his own creation.

> "We two," he tells Lacombe in the letter of the 11th of
> March, 1867, "speak the same language, a strange language,
> alas, to most of those who think themselves artists. Our
> ideas are in principle the same."

Allowing for the fact that Lacombe was more
promising than most students, one detects in
such words an absence of the celestial, condes-
cending manner, which is second nature to not a
few professors. Even when the mentor has to
take exception to an idea or a modulation he does
so in a manner that is almost aplogetic. An
example of this meets one in the second letter of
the set. Speaking of a composition by Lacombe,
he describes it as

> "flabby and spiritless. The theme is short. It has not
> enough poetry for the dream-picture you sought. There is,
> without doubt, a certain languor, a certain charm in the piece
> as a whole, but not enough. Obviously it is not bad, but you
> ought, you are able, to do better. Believe me. My judg-
> ment will appear severe to you. Wait a little while. Put
> your piece away and, when you look at it again after having
> almost forgotten it, you will be of my opinion. You will
> find it almost a soap bubble. . . . I have always observed
> that the least satisfactory compositions are the ones most
> cherished at the time of hatching. I fear things which are
> like improvisations."

He sums up an andante thus : " It is *good*, but

not very good." A piece that does not touch his heart, that has the perfume of 1830, or even of 1829, and reminds him of a horrible patriotic song which filled the streets in 1848, and because of this association renders it difficult for him to judge it on its merits, is finally summarised in this way : " Altogether, without being enthusiastic about this melody I find in it the touch of the musician and of the intelligent thinker. It is better than ninety-nine hundredths of the melodies in vogue." When he runs across something which appeals to him, he is far from stingy in his praise. An intermezzo is " worthy of a master ; " Lacombe is " a symphonist ; " an andante is " *en plein* Beethoven ! " " Is it the orchestra which frightens you ? " he asks. " How stupid ! You know how to score, I tell you. *It is your duty to write a symphony.*" A few lines further down he pens these words : " The close above all is very pleasing. The development goes well." Other remarks as enthusiastic can be found elsewhere in the Lacombe letters.

Knowledge of Bizet as a teacher can be increased by a perusal of Galabert's pages. When Galabert decided to take lessons Bizet asked him whether he read, and if so, what books. The young man, who had read both French and foreign authors, told Bizet. " That settles it," said the composer. " People think that one has no need to be cultured to be a musician ; they are wrong ; on the contrary, it is necessary to know many things."

Writing to Galabert, in July or August, 1865, he reproached his friend with being an " austere philosopher." " Fortify yourself with *Don Giovanni, The Marriage of Figaro, The Magic Flute, Cosi fan tutte.* Scrutinise Weber also." Another pupil pays handsome tribute to Bizet's teaching gifts. " I remember very well," this pupil informs me, " that he was a marvellous pianist and and admirable teacher, as he taught me harmony in one month from a little book, *Le Traité de Catel,* which, he said, was quite enough for a person with a musical nature. I took my last lesson three days before his death, when he was in bed quite depressed and broken-hearted over the enormous failure of *Carmen* ! "

In speaking of the musicians with whom at one time or another our subject rubbed shoulders, I ought, surely, to give pride of place to Marmontel and Halévy, who directed the steps of the youth. The relationship which existed between Marmontel and his favourite student can be gathered from the professor's sketch in his volume, *Symphonistes et Virtuosos.* In the presence of Marmontel, Bizet did not feel the restraint that so often takes hold of a student when he faces his instructor. Indeed, the old piano teacher, who often saw Bizet at his brightest and breeziest, appreciated him in his boyish moments quite as much as in his more serious ones. Of Halévy, it is scarcely necessary to say a great deal here. I have already spoken of the esteem with which each regarded the other. Bizet looked up to Halévy, and Halévy rejoiced in the successes of his pupil, as, for example, when he showed Liszt of what stuff he was made. A few years after Halévy's death, the young fellow married that master's daughter, while a pious sentiment caused him to undertake the completing of *Noë*.

The name of Ernest Guiraud should next be written down, because Guiraud, almost of the same age as Bizet, was his closest friend. " I am delighted with Guiraud's prize", wrote Bizet to Marmontel, when he heard that this comrade in arms had won the *prix de Rome*," he is a true musician." Guiraud, in his turn, reached the Eternal City and Bizet was delighted : " he is lovable, modest, frank and loyal. We have the same musical ideas".[1] It was no time till they were playing piano duets together. The two men were inseparable. They consulted one another about their compositions and often worked at the same table.[2] What Guiraud's counsel meant will, perhaps, never be known. So long as Guiraud existed, Bizet lacked not a true and faithful friend ; he was certainly a stout champion, a strong supporter. No taint of jealousy marred the close relationship ; each rejoiced in the successes of the other ; each felt that the other understood him ; each had the utmost confidence in the other's judgment. A

[1] Letter of 3rd of February 1860.
[2] Galabert.

mutual admiration and an identity of tastes and interests furnished a twofold bond to be sundered only by death.

For Saint-Saëns Bizet had a great liking. There is an amusing story about the author of *Samson and Delilah* that is characteristic of that exceedingly resourceful man. Bizet's father had a house at Vesinet, to which the family generally repaired in the month of May. One summer evening, when the composer was writing in his room there, he heard a tenor voice sing the romance from *Les Pêcheurs de Perles*. He went into the garden, and saw someone coming along the road. It was Saint-Saëns, who, not knowing the Bizet dwelling, adopted this means of arousing the attention of his colleague.[1] The death of the younger was for the older composer a cruel blow. Long afterwards, Saint-Saëns remembered going one day to Croissy, and there hearing Bizet play the first number of the second act of *Carmen*, just composed, which amazed him. When they last met—it was in the Place de la Madeleine— Bizet congratulated Saint-Saëns on the success which had attended the production of the symphonic poem, *Phaëton*. It may be noted in passing that Saint-Saëns transcribed for the piano a number from *Les Pêcheurs de Perles*.

Of Massenet, who composed the elegaic *lamento*, Galabert heard Bizet say nothing that was not favourable. The passing allusion to

[1] Galabert.

163

the man which Massenet introduces into his volume of souvenirs is entirely sympathetic in manner. Ernest. Reyer understood and sympathised with the musician who was more sure of himself and had a more prodigious memory than any other he had known.[1] There remains Auber, the dapper little fellow, the manufacturer of *bons mots*, who controlled the destinies of the Conservatoire when the bright stripling first entered its portals. Bizet's attitude towards Auber was not one of unmeasured admiration : it might, perhaps, with accuracy be called one of aversion. He did not look upon Auber as a perfect director of the Conservatoire, nor did he look upon him, I think, as a very great musician : " Saint-Saëns, Guiraud, Massenet, myself, and some others might be able to rejuvenate this school of which Monsieur Auber has made such a disreputable institution that I cannot properly describe it."[2] An excellent tale is on record concerning a meeting which took place between Auber and Bizet. The former's *La Fiancée du Roi de Garbe* followed *Les Pêcheurs de Perles* at an interval of a few months, *Le Premier Jour de Bonheur* ran hard upon the heels of *La Jolie Fille de Perth*. At the time of those double appearances, the old master ran up against the young one. " Ah ! " said Auber in a formal manner, " I have heard your work. It is good, very

[1] *Les Debats*, 13th June 1875.
[2] Letter to Mme. Halévy, April 1871.

good." " I accept your congratulations," answered Bizet, " but I am unable to return them." A grimace on Auber's part was met with a further comment by the younger man : " A simple soldier may receive the congratulations of a marshal of France ; he is not able to offer them to him."[1] The way in which Bizet refers to Monsieur Auber has no doubt its own significance. In leaving this subject, I must not fail to direct the reader's attention to Marmontel's praise of Bizet's frank acknowledgment of the merits of others. The professor possessed letters wherein the pupil spoke with enthusiasm of his comrades and his colleagues.

Some people will agree, others will disagree, with the writer who declares that Bizet had incontestable literary gifts. The published letters appear to me to be of value chiefly because they are natural. In reading them we seem to see the composer himself and hear him talking to us. As a rule, he comes to the point without ado. With infinite zest, he rattles off his ideas, and with abruptness changes the topic. When he took up the pen to write prose he wanted to satisfy a desire as modest as it is common ; he wanted to say something, and what he wanted to say, he said with as little palaver as possible. Once or twice, his manner of expression might be described as telegrammatic. He wrote quickly, I imagine, and without any thought of publicaion .

[1] Galabert.

He had not, as some letter-writers have, an eye upon a future audience. He addressed himself to the addressee, not to the occupant of an imaginary stall or gallery. He never gave a moment's thought to posterity. Here and there, an illegible word has successfully baffled even a painstaking editor, which implies that Bizet ran through his correspondence as expeditiously as he could. This belief is further substantiated by the absence of any rhetorical or poetical flights. It was never his aim to set down a passage that would impart a thrill by reason of its style ; or, if it were, which I gravely doubt, he never managed to do so. Perhaps he knew his limitations, and, the words coming quickly to his pen, he traced them on the paper, giving no thought to the polishing process beloved of the fastidious. As a whole, the letters disclose a man who is very interested in all that is going on around him. He freely opens his mind and, though obviously of a warm heart, does not hesitate to call a spade a spade.

One critic has taken exception to the publication of the letters that Bizet wrote as a young man. The making known of them this critic calls " the cruellest blow that has been given to his memory " and a "veritable sacrilege."[1] The accessibility of the letters in question is little likely to cause uneasiness to a generation which so often puts its friends up to auction by joyfully recording their private conversation in order to pocket a publisher's

[1] Gauthier-Villars.

cheque. As it happens, the student of Bizet's life has at his elbow a not inconsiderable number of letters which he can peruse, and he will find, unless I am mistaken, that a careful perusal adds materially to his knowledge of the man ; for in these pages Bizet is discovered. Music and musicians, of course, bulk largely, and his own projects occupy a liberal amount of space. But, apart from what may, without disrespect, be called " shop talk ", there remain his comments on men and affairs, political events and other subjects ; and I believe it is worth while to fill in the lines of the portrait by considering, however briefly, the commentator upon miscellaneous and divers themes.

More than once, after looking about him he says what he thinks of the conditions of France. Shortly after the débâcle, in April, 1871, for example, he writes to Mme. Halévy that he hopes the good government which is at the moment in power will consolidate and purify the arts, as there is great need for it. Presumably by way of consoling the same lady, he informs her soon after that the calamitous times through which they are passing are not unprecedented in French history, and adds that it is always astonishing to the spectator to see how the nation, plunged in the abyss, recovers itself almost at once. The siege of Paris by Henry IV, he reminds her, was one of the worst times for Paris. Six months after, the country had attained to a degree of prosperity

that it has perhaps never known since, notwithstanding the immense progress of civilization.[1]

A tilt at the Parisian public assumes this form ;
" The cosmopolitan public which we have the
honour to possess in Paris at this moment runs
after celebrated names, not new works."[2] After
repeating the words " without form no style,
without style no art," he quotes Buffon ap-
provingly.[3] A passage which occurs at the end
of a letter of January 1867 will interest the
English reader : " Continue to dig into Shakespeare. He is good. He is a philosopher, a
moralist and poet." Here and there nippy
touches are to be found. Consider this little
example of sarcasm dispatched from Rome :
" Schnetz alone is received into Italian society ;
but he is Italian through and through. He has
lived twenty years in Italy and has studied the
interests and tastes of Italians so far as never to
wash his hands."[4] In the same letter, we read
of the painters who are always divided into two
camps—the colourists and the designers : " Unhappily, the colourists do not know more of colour
than the designers, and the designers are as
ignorant of design as the colourists." To Marmontel he avows his dislike of trivialities : " I have
a horror of this ' petite musiquette'. To the devil with
all those people who see in our sublime art only

[1] Letter of 12th of May 1871.
[2] Letter of October 1867.
[3] Letter of October 1866.
[4] Letter of the 16th of May 1858.

an innocent tickling of the ear." When asked to write religious music, he agreed to do so, but it would be of the pagan religion. *Carmen seculare* of Horace seemed to him better from a literary and poetic point of view than the words of the Mass. Talking on this subject, he made the confession that he was more pagan than Christian.[1] He liked none too well the ceremonial of the Church, as is very evident from the outspoken remarks to be found in a letter written to his mother in April, 1858 ; while his views on religion occupy a great portion of an epistle inscribed to Galabert in October, 1866, where he is very emphatic in stating his case. Those who read these two passages will find that Bizet could lay forth with considerable force. " Happily," he observes, when writing to his father from Naples on the 24th of October, 1859, " one is able to love God without loving the curés ! " I have quoted the foregoing scattered remarks, as I venture to think that they bring us into close contact with the man himself, and I hope that the reading of them will encourage a study of the whole correspondence. In going through the letters, it is, however, very necessary to bear in mind that Bizet was a temperamental man.

Once, and once only, so far as I have been able to discover, did Bizet hold the critic's pen in hand. In 1867, he accepted the position of music critic to *La Revue Nationale et Etrangère*,

[1] Letter of the 20th of March 1860.

an important publication among whose contributors were some celebrated men. An article written by him appeared in the issue of the 3rd of August, 1867, under the nom de plume, Gaston de Betzi. It proved to be his solitary contribution. The reason which lies at the back of the singular circumstance remains something of a mystery. By his own confession, he set out to undertake what every person, who has, however modestly, engaged in musical criticism will agree to be an enormously difficult task. He set out to tell the truth, all the truth, and nothing but the truth. " I have nothing to do with any coterie," he writes, " I have only friends who will cease to be my friends the day they no longer respect my free will, my complete independence," which is the right, the only attitude to take up. One or two of the views contained in the article deserve to be mentioned. " Composers are becoming rare, but, on the other hand, parties and sets multiply without end." He is evidently amused at the cult of exoticism : " We have French, German and Italian music, and, in addition, Russian, Hungarian and Polish music, etc. ; without counting Arab, Japanese and Tunisian music, all three very much in favour since the opening of the Universal Exhibition. . . . We have, again, melodic music, harmonic music, learned music, the most dangerous of all." " Is it necessary to decry Molière in order to like Shakespeare ? Is genius not of all countries, of all time ? " " The composer," he goes on to say, " gives the best of himself to the making of a work ; he believes, doubts, becomes enthusiastic, despairs, rejoices and suffers in turn ; when, more apprehensive than a criminal, he comes with it and says ' See and judge', instead of letting it affect us, we ask for his passport. We inquire about his opinions, his relations, and artistic antecedents." For Bizet this was not criticism ; it was to play the rôle of policeman. " The artist has neither label nor nationality ; he is inspired or he is not ; he has, or has not, genius or talent." Thus laying about him in words which do not lack emphasis, he warns his readers against the habit of asking from a great artist the things he lacks. " Know how to profit from those he possesses."

I have referred in general terms to the works the composer thought of but did not write, commenced to write but did not finish, and finished but withheld from publicity. In all artistic creation there is necessarily a considerable amount of waste. The creator fastens upon an idea around which his thoughts play only to find that it is less rich potentially, less amenable to treatment, than he had supposed in the first moment of ecstatic embrace. The acceptance and rejection will be more frequent with some men than with others, because all men do not work in the same way. As I have hinted, there is evidence that the adoption and discarding of a subject was not a rare occurrence with Bizet. Gaston Magny puts it thus : " The works burned and left incomplete constitute a considerable baggage." It is no exaggeration to say that ninety-nine out of every hundred people who know *Carmen* are ignorant of the names of the pieces belonging to the category of the unfinished and lost.

Writing to Marmontel, Bizet speaks of an opera in four acts, called *Esmeralda*, based on Victor Hugo, a title which recalls Goring Thomas. It was to have been his second *envoi* from Rome, but he changed his mind and wrote *Vasco da Gama* instead. There are references to *Esmeralda* in the letters which he wrote from Italy under the dates, 30th of October and 31st of December, 1858. In the summer of 1859 he was persuaded that a musician ought to find his own subject-matter, and to this end he has been busy. " Get *Hoffmann's Tales* and read *Le Tonnelier de Nuremberg*. I wish to write three acts on this delicious poem," he writes on the 4th of June. A few weeks later he returns to the topic. Almost at the same time, on the 24th of October, 1859, he speaks of his having been wrapped up in the idea of a *Don Quichotte, tragi-heroï-comique*." Early in the following year, the 20th of March, 1860, he commences *L'Amour Peintre* by Molière.

Just before the war of 1870, he was for a while immersed in an opéra-comique in three acts called *Calendal*, a book by Paul Ferrier, which was given up, as du Locle did not care for the subject. The ninth letter to Lacombe shows that the composer liked the poem. Soon after, he took up *Clarissa Harlowe*, a book in three acts based on Richardson. Of this, too, he seems to have been enamoured. One act, it is said, had taken definite shape in his mind, and some jottings were discovered after his death.[1] With *Clarissa Harlowe* ought to be bracketed *Grisélidis*, libretto by Sardou and du Locle in three acts, as it belongs to the same period. He calls it " a charming piece,"[2] and writes on the 26th of February, 1871, that it is " very advanced." He also took on hand *Les Templiers*, a grand opera in five acts by Léon Halévy. *Le Cid* was brought to such a point that he could play it to his friends, but he played it only from rough sketches which meant nothing to others.[3] " I have composed this summer a *Cid* in five acts", he tells Lacombe.[4] Guiraud found both beauty and power in it.

At the time of his death Bizet thought of striking out upon an entirely new line, that of oratorio. Louis Gallet had written a libretto, the title of which is variously given as *Geneviève de Paris*, *Geneviève*, *Patronne de Paris*, and *Sainte Geneviève*. According to Octave Séré, no number of it had been put on paper, though it is possible a few bars had actually been traced.[5]

[1] Pigot.
[2] Letter to Galabert, June 1870.
[3] Tiersot.
[4] Twentieth letter, 1874 (?)
[5] Pigot.

After intimating that he finishes *Carmen*, Bizet tells Lacombe that he is beginning *Sainte Geneviève*, an oratorio on which he counts much. It was destined for the Concerts Lamoureux. Mention of an oratorio may cause surprise to the reader, but Tiersot's words provide a plausible explanation. The success which Massenet had gained with *Marie Magdeleine* (1873) may not have been without its influence;[1] and, perhaps, as the French critic observes, the example of César Franck's *Redemption* (1873) was not lost upon Bizet. The same writer describes the scheme in these words : " A series of musical tableaux showing the predestined child, then the noble woman devoted to her people, succouring the fugitives driven from their homes by the invasion of the barbarians, strengthening the courage of the Parisians, and, sublime miracle, triumphing over Attila by the power of her faith." It is a pity, thinks Tiersot, that, in place of two works, French music did not almost simultaneously produce a trilogy, conceived in oratorio form, but different spiritually. " It is necessary to insist," he writes, " on the significance of this work which does not exist . . . it would, without doubt, have been a masterpiece and have disclosed to us a new aspect of the genius of the author."

For the rest, it may be said that two numbers

[1] Bizet cordially congratulated Massenet on the production of *Marie Magdeleine*.

composed for *La Jolie Fille de Perth* were suppressed—a romance and a duet ;[1] and that there
is enthusiastic mention of a symphony, based on
the *Lusiade* of Camoëns, in the letters of the
3rd of August 1859 and the 17th of January
1860, both addressed to Marmontel. Three
works which evidently went to make a bonfire
have been spoken of ; they are *La Guzla de
l'Emir, Ivan le Terrible* and *La Coupe du Roi de
Thulé*. A piece composed about 1868 or 1869,
and carried to a finish, can most fitly be disposed
of here, as it has disappeared. It was a vaudeville operetta called *Sol-si-ré-pif-pan*, written to
words by William Busnach, and was presented at
the Menus Plaisirs. As Bizet did not put his
name to the score, I fancy that he was not very
proud of it. Like a good friend, Guiraud scanned
the sketches and fragments which escaped destruction, and, no doubt, tried his utmost to make
something of such modest hints. If he could not
bring back the power and beauty Bizet had
captured in *Le Cid*, if he could not construct
another score to be heard at length within the
walls of the theatre, the task, we may take it, was
beyond all men. The next chapter of activity
was to have been one which told of *Le Cid* at
the Opéra and *Sainte Geneviève* at the Lamoureux
Concerts. The Fates intervened. The music
of *Le Cid* was lost to the world ; *Sainte Geneviève*
remains merely a name.

[1] Galabert.

CHAPTER IV

Period of Bizet's Productivity—A survey of his works—*Don Procopio*—*Les Pêcheurs de Perles*—France and Exoticism—*La Jolie Fille de Perth*—A one-act opera and its Libretto—Its Eastern note—The crowning glory of *Carmen*—Mérimée's book and the plot—The story as told by Meilhac and Halévy—The character of Carmen—Don José often misinterpreted—Escamillo the Victorious—Two views of Micaela—Spanish Music ?—No real break with tradition—Dual aspect of story emphasised in the score—Comments upon the music—*L'Arlésienne* and its Provençal Airs—*Roma*—*Patrie* overture—Bizet's piano music and songs—Bizet and the Wagner question—His place among the Masters of Music.

BIZET'S career as a composer may be said to have begun in 1863, the year in which *Les Pêcheurs de Perles* was produced. As it terminated with *Carmen*, it lasted for only twelve years. The term was brief, but those who have thought much about questions of art will not, on that account, be deceived. If fifty years of Europe are better than a cycle of Cathay, twelve years of activity may be far more impressive, far more interesting than many times their number spent in idle days. Life is not to be measured by its length, but by its intensity.

The period during which Bizet took his place

176

among the composers of France is a period to
which the student is likely to be attracted   The
star of Meyerbeer, whose posthumous *L'Africaine*
came out in 1865, had begun to set, even if his
influence were to linger and his name to be
remembered for some years to come.   Berlioz's
Les Troyens à Carthage did not make a great success
when produced in 1863.   Auber, a veteran of
many years' standing, wrote *La Fiancée du Roi des
Garbes, Le Premier Jour de Bonheur* and *Le
Rêve d'Amour*. Gounod was prominent, *Philémon
et Baucis, La Reine de Saba, Mireille* and *Roméo
et Juilette* following one another in quick succession.   Ambroise Thomas's most popular opera,
Mignon, made its début in 1866, and this he
followed up with the version of *Hamlet* which
Bizet so much admired.   In the midst of the
illustrious company sat a former violoncellist of
the Opéra Comique, who now poured out with
amazing ease and swiftness a series of light works,
to which the cynical, flippant, and frivolous
society of the second Empire, fond of the topical
allusion, the witty stroke, and the art of the
caricaturist, lent a willing ear.

To the general chorus some of the younger
voices added their notes.   Saint-Saëns composed
a series of symphonic poems during the 'seventies;
Massenet began a long and successful career
with *La Grand' Tante* and *Don César de Bazan*.
Delibes proved the possession of a delicate touch
in *Le Roi l'a dit* in 1873, though the perfect

177

charm of his art was to be disclosed only three years later with *Sylvia*. Sarasate played Lalo's violin concerto (Op. 20) with great success in the year 1874. And there was Bizet. How did he comport himself ; what sort of figure did he cut ? Let us look first at the operas.

I have spoken of *Les Pêcheurs de Perles* as the starting point, for *Don Procopio* belongs to the days of studentship, and is therefore, in the strict sense of the phrase, *hors d'oeuvre*. Nevertheless, a word or two concerning this *opéra-bouffe* may not be out of place. It has been told how Bizet came upon the subject when he visited a second-hand bookstall in Rome. The Italian farce which he then unearthed came from the pen of Gambaggio. The score disappeared in Paris and was taken for lost. In 1895 Auber's heirs restored to Weckerlin, then librarian of the Paris Conservatoire, several compositions in manuscript written by holders of the *prix de Rome*, which had somehow got mixed up with the papers left by the old composer. Among them were two hundred and thirty-six pages of full score in Bizet's handwriting. The music was neatly written, and—an important matter—there were no erasures. While no date was affixed, the title on the first page, read *Don Procopio, opera buffa in due atti*. The score was intact except for the recitatives, which Charles Malherbe, who had discovered the piece, supplied, while Paul Collin and Paul Bérel reconstructed the libretto.

As published, the work consists of twelve numbers and an *entr'acte*. The words printed on the title page—"after the Italian comedies of the 17th and 18th centuries"—faithfully indicate its nature and its style ; and a quotation from a letter of Bizet, reproduced in the score, briefly explains how the music came to be as it is : "*Sur les paroles Italiennes it faut faire Italien ; je n'ai pas cherché a me dérober a cette influence.*"

The action passes in Italy about the year 1800, and there are seven characters. The dramatic stuff itself is of the lightest. Bettina is loved by a gallant young officer called Odoardo, and fools her old uncle, Andronico, who keeps an eagle eye upon her. Andronico presents to his niece the inevitable *vieil avare* in the person of Procopio. Procopio, however, is made to believe that the charming Bettina's failings lie in her poverty, her flightiness, and her extravagant tastes. One does not need to be told how it all turns out. Ultimately Andronico, in obedience to the laws which govern this type of work, holds out his hand to Odoardo, and the well-known clinching formula, "*Amants soyez unis*," leads at once to the final jollification, which obligingly allows people to draw their cloaks around them and put away their opera-glasses.

The music is facile, melodious and very Italian, and it shows that Bizet had read and re-read his Rossini. The very first bars, in fact, recall a passage to be found at the beginning of

Il Barbiere, and Rossinian is the only adjective to be applied to that part of the duet between Bettina and Procopio which starts at page 183 of the score ; those reiterated thirds might have leapt from the fluent pen of the Swan of Pesaro. Bizet's own confession inclines one to the belief that he did not tax his resources very greatly in writing the piece. He allowed the music to make itself. He enjoyed the composition of a work in the genre of Donizetti's *Don Pasquale* ; he enjoyed the recreation all the more because he loved the smiling, sparkling art of the South, with its suave themes and tripping measures. The Italian influence was strong upon him. He readily submitted to it, and the submission implies a disinclination to project his own personality into the music. He neither confronted himself with, nor sought the solution of, subtle points. It was enough for him that he basked in the Italian sun and enjoyed the heat of its beneficent rays. Only in one or two diminutive touches does the physiognomy of the later Bizet appear. The adoption of the little military march theme, with its *pianissimo* entrance and its staccato manner, seems to me characteristic, as Bizet always had a liking for the light-stepping, brief and rhythmic subject, that lends itself to deft instrumental handling. And the last four bars of the ninth number, with the repetition of the thirds in four octaves, are similarly typical of him. Gauthier-Villars notes that some of the chorus work in

Act I reappears in *Les Pêcheurs de Perles* ; it may
be added that the serenade which opens Act II
figures also in *La Jolie Fille de Perth*.   Like all
works of this class, *Don Procopio* needs good singing.   The ensembles will fall flat unless they are
skilfully rendered, as for instance at the " *écouter* "
and " *allons* " on page 29, and the composer
presumes a clean and reliable technique on the
part of his solo singers.   As a repository of ideas
the little opera does not take high rank, but it
should run along pleasantly in the theatre if it
be nimbly and crisply performed.   It is easy to
break this butterfly music on the wheel of the
grand opera manner.

Les Pêcheurs de Perles is a much more ambitious
affair.   Italian through and through, *Don Procopio* was written by a man, who, for the moment,
assumed the garb of the South and raised his
voice willingly in Italian song.   *Les Pêcheurs
de Perles* takes one to Ceylon.   In writing it
Bizet made the first of many imaginative journeys,
a fact which has not escaped one, at least, of his
French critics, who likens the composer to a
globe-trotter of the end of the second Empire and
a commercial traveller dealing in French music.
Artistically speaking, Bizet certainly compassed
much ground.   Italy was followed by Ceylon ;
La Jolie Fille de Perth is Scottish, in origin at
least ; *Djamileh* necessitates a visit to Egypt ;
L'Arlésienne calls us to Provence, and *Carmen*,
as all the world knows, plays itself out in Spain.

Bizet had, therefore, plenty of opportunity for meditating upon the value and efficacy of local colour.

It is not surprising, I think, that this opera, the first considerable work which the composer undertook, should be concerned with the East. I do not know what prompted the adoption of the subject, but I surmise that Félicien David's symphonic ode *Le Désert*, which, with its call of the muezzin, dance of the almées and prayer to Allah, caused a stir when it was produced in 1844, had not been forgotten, and that the European success won by it was not lost upon the artistic adventurers who, like Alexander of old, longed for new worlds to conquer. Even if the excitement stimulated by David's ode had exhausted itself, one need not hold up one's hands in astonishment, either at Ceylon on the stage or at Bizet's imaginative peregrinations. The themes which he set were provided for him. It almost seems as if those who presented him with his texts were anxious to submit him to a life-long examination on the subject of local colour. But, in writing music for these various texts, widely contrasted as they are spiritually and geographically, he stood shoulder to shoulder with his confrères. If we are drawn to the series of works which begins with *Les Pêcheurs de Perles* and ends with *Carmen*, we shall find that the attraction does not lie merely in the changes of latitude and temperature, though we are conscious of them.

It is both foolish and misleading to speak as if
Bizet had been a commercial traveller advertising
French music at the ends of the earth, if by so
doing one means to imply that he was engaged in
an unique occupation. If the simile be at all per-
missible, which is very doubtful, its application to a
very large number of composers can in no wise
provoke objection. By dwelling now in Italy, now
in Ceylon, now in Egypt, and again in Provence
and Spain, he was not abandoning himself to
an unique eccentricity. Much more curious
would it have been had Fate denied him those
frequent sojourns far from the boulevards of
Paris.

This will be allowed if we remember the
paradox which lies at the root of so much French
art. In his *Honorine* Balzac contrasts the French
and the English. If the French, he says, have
an aversion for travelling and the English a love
for it, both nations have good reasons to offer.
Something better than England is everywhere to
be found ; it is difficult to find the charms of
France abroad. Balzac's words tell us what we
all know. The French are a home-loving people,
never so happy as when walking the streets of
their own towns, gazing upon their own landscapes, and hearing their own tongue. But if an
enormous appreciation of the charms and delights
of a country at once charming and delightful
keeps the average Frenchman from travelling
as much as the Englishman, the American, or

the German, many of the most imaginative and sensitive of his countrymen have looked beyond the horizon to find sights wondrous beautiful to their keen vision. Balzac's Marquis d'Espard laboured at a " picturesque history of China," and his Gambara waxed enthusiastic over the great opera, *Mahomet*. The labours of those fictitious personages do not lack significance, for their like is to be found in real life. Le Sage, for example, reflected the influence of Calderon, and started his career with a couple of plays in which he emulated Lope de Vega. According to Anatole France, Chateaubriand " was the first to infuse exoticism into poetry and make it ferment there." De Musset attracted attention with his *Contes d'Espagnes et d'Italie*. The de Goncourts fell under the spell of Japanese art. Flaubert's *Salammbô* recounts the struggle between Rome and Carthage ; and it should not be necessary to sing the praises of that master-piece, *Thaïs*. Much as he loves France, much as he is tempted to remain there, the cultured French-man often responds readily and fruitfully to alien influences ; and when he does go abroad, as Félicien David, Lamartine, Gautier and Mérimée did, it is to return rich in ideas. He may, thinking of the irksomeness of travel and the beauties of his own country, hesitate to undertake the physical journey ; he seldom hesitates to undertake the imaginative one. Magic carpets have fewer terrors than the most luxurious liner, and one can go far upon them without parting from home comforts.

It is not difficult to find in the ranks of French musicians analogues of the literary men just named. Camille Bellaigue speaks of " *la France historique et la France exotique.*" The latter is important. Félicien David's *Le Désert* must have seemed to many like a golden key which opened the door leading to sweet-smelling gardens. But David, after all, was only one of the many French composers destined to quench their thirst for the new and strange at oriental springs ; and this fact should be kept in mind when we glance at the titles of Bizet's works. If Bizet were a commercial traveller turning up one moment in Ceylon and another in Spain, what is to be said of the polymathic Saint-Saëns with his chameleon-like adaptability ; of Saint-Saëns, who wrote *La Princesse Jaune*, Persian songs, an Algerian suite, an African fantasia, a havanaise, an Arab caprice, and souvenirs of Italy and Lisbon ? And what is to be said of Massenet, who eagerly seized the opportunities to indulge in exoticism which came his way ; of Massenet, who provided the divertissement in *Le Roi de Lahore*, the Moorish rhapsody and ballet of the Spanish Provinces in *Le Cid*, and Dulcinea's song with guitar accompaniment in *Don Quichotte?* What is to be said of Reyer, Lalo, Chabrier and Delibes, and the picturesque march of César Franck's camel drivers ? Surely, it is not a nine days' wonder that Bizet, in the few years of his creative life, was urged by the librettists and the managers to hie him away to far parts. It would, all things considered, have been infinitely more astonishing if he had not been invited to visit them.

This becomes more obvious when one looks at the matter a little more closely. We have seen that Bizet, in that whimsical way of his, twitted those who made much of exoticism and particularly those aspects of it, Arabian, Japanese, and Tunisian which the Paris Exhibition of 1867 had apparently been instrumental in bringing into prominence. But the origin of the cult goes further back, and has no connection with " Wembleyism " in any shape or form. If it would be too much to claim that exoticism was a direct legacy of the Romantic movement, it is hardly too much to claim that it received from that movement, and especially from the French manifestation of it, a potent stimulus. Like all movements, the Romantic revival was a passive protest transformed by intensity of feeling and conviction into an active campaign. Among its general distinguishing features were a restoration of folk literature, ballad and legend, a renewal of interest in the remote, whether of time or place, a glorification of the Middle Age, and a desire for local colour, that Brunetière described as " a literary acquisition of Romanticism." The wheels of chivalry were set vehemently in motion. Romanticists longed for " the roses of Shiraz "

and looked beyond the frontiers ; distance lent a
very great enchantment ; far-off times were seen
in a rosy light ; the luxurious gardens of the
South, the spice-laden groves of the East were
very pleasant to their gaze ; and rustic flutings
fell gently upon their willing ears. The link
which unites exoticism to the Romantic movement is to be discovered in a curiosity of spirit
that will take no denial. If the romanticist
dreamt of the years that were and dwelt in
distant lands, the exoticist sailed the seas and
returned home heavy-laden. It is to curiosity
allied to a love of beauty that we owe exoticism
in music, which might not inaptly be termed a
discovery of the world as a musical asset.

To return to *Les Pêcheurs de Perles.* The
plot must be set down as a very poor one. There
are people, I am aware, who do not lay much
stress upon the subject-matter or the words of an
opera. To them an opera is so much music.
If they find the music agreeable, they are not
inclined to trouble about either plot or lines. The
attitude is a luxurious one, which no serious critic
dare assume. Music may be the predominant
partner in all operas : it is, nevertheless, allied
to plots and libretti on which it is commonly
presumed to throw some light. An opera must
be regarded as a whole, because complexity in the
plot, or dullness in the words is likely to affect its
career and throw a dark shadow over the score.
Both plot and words are vitally important, though

one often wonders if makers of plots and scrib-
blers of words realise the fact. The example of
Il Trovatore comes to mind. This plot has for
many years been a laughing-stock, and some
enterprising individual ought to offer a prize to
the person who can, in reasonable compass, give a
lucid account of what is supposed to happen on
the stage. The sheer power of music to obtain
acceptance for what otherwise would be consigned
to the dustbin has never been more startlingly
exhibited than in this early Verdi work. After
hearing it, and thus realising the vital power of
music, we can well believe that had Schubert set
an advertisement to music, as someone said he
could have done, the advertisement might have
been assured of immortality. Without the music,
Il Trovatore would be simply unbearable.

The fundamental weakness of *Les Pêcheurs de
Perles* is one not lightly to be dismissed. It
arises both from the nature of the theme and the
the characters to whom we are introduced.
Speaking for myself, I find in neither the com-
pelling attraction, which, by engaging the attention from the start, wins half the operatic battle.
I do not care two straws what happens to any of
the characters. I am too conscious of the man
who pulls the wires and makes his marionettes go
through their little antics to be greatly moved.
Leïla, Zurga, Nadir and the rest are to me stage
puppets, lacking the breath of life, and, as such, of
very small concern.

The story works a triangle motif, though not quite the triangle motif which has been described as the one French plot. Zurga and his comrade, Nadir, are haunted by the recollection of a beautiful and mysterious person whom they once saw at Kandy. They try to forget the love which she kindled in their hearts, because it threatened to turn their friendship into rivalry. A veiled priestess, who comes to invoke protection for the pearl fishers, approaches. She calls on the mighty Brahma. Nadir recognises in Leïla, for it is she, the mysterious divinity who captured his affections, and is enraptured when she recognises him. These two meet and proclaim their love. Nourabad, the High Priest, overhears them, and in his rage demands that justice shall be meted out. Zurga, being chief of the tribe, has the last word, but, remembering that Nadir is his friend, would temper the severity of the verdict. Nourabad, tearing the veil from the face of the woman, reveals Leïla, whom Nadir had sworn to renounce. Zurga condemns the lovers to death. Leïla pleads for Nadir ; for herself she has no fear. As the sentence is about to be carried out, an alarm that the camp is on fire is raised. The assembled crowd rushes off to stem the disaster. Zurga owns that the fire was originated by him and sets free the condemned couple. Nourabad, who appears to be something of a detective, has seen through Zurga's manoeuvre and denounces him to the people. Leïla having escaped, Zurga

himself must burn at the stake. The work terminates with a hymn to Brahma.

Only music very far removed from the ordinary
could carry all this successfully upon its back, and,
to be quite frank, the music of *Les Pêcheurs de
Perles* is not so very far removed from the ordinary.
I am not inclined to deny that it has its own
interest and attraction ; but that interest and
attraction are very largely of the historical order.
In it we see a document that records progress,
gives us some idea of the place Bizet occupied in
1863, and shows how far he had attained mastery
over his own powers at that date. The score
has more power than originality. Indeed, it
resembles some of the early scores of Verdi in
that it indicates a greater power than the composer knew profitably how to employ. While
the power is not by any means of the first rank,
its presence is felt, but one feels still more acutely
that Bizet had not yet learned how to make the
most of his resources. A certain scrappiness,
which betokens mental restlessness, a young
man's natural desire to avoid monotony, and a
disability, or disinclination, to settle down and
exhaust a thematic seam will be noticed. The
prevailing style is far from revolutionary. The
little prelude, extracted from the first act (the
entrance of Leïla), takes the form of a sweet and
languishing melody in the manner of Gounod,
which, once given out, is repeated an octave
higher. There is not much distinction in the

choruses for all their animation, though the invocation, " *Brahma, divin Brahma,*" with its breadth and simplicity, is operatically effective in a rather obvious way. One chorus, that associated with Leïla's " *Dans le ciel sans voile*", is of such unspeakable banality that it aroused the anger of Berlioz. The solos own an allegiance to Italy, which is not purchased without the sacrifice of character. What should have been one of the best numbers, Leïla's cavatina, is innocent of this desirable attribute. At the end of it, as at the end of her air in the first act, there is the inevitable cascade of notes on the impressive and highly significant word, " ah ! " (How would the older opera-makers have managed without the " ah " and " is " to help them out at the critical moment, when the song-bird takes her flight ?) As for the exoticism, it is of course intermittent—operatic exoticism is bound to be so ; but it is also of the facile variety, and might easily, one imagines, have been made to play a more important and more effective part. As a matter of fact, the alien note is never sounded other than very modestly. It appears in the opening chorus, in Leïla's " *O Dieu Brahma* " with chorus " off," and in Nadir's solo " *A mon amie*", with its distant harp. Curiously enough, the call to Brahma already referred to is not couched in exotic vein.

The way in which Bizet has returned to the melody that first appears in the duet for Nadir and

Zurga, wherein they sing of the haunting figure
they have seen, forms one of the best features of
the work. This theme first recurs immediately
after Leïla's entrance (*p.p.p. tremolo*), where it
furnishes a background for the suppressed ejacu-
ations on the part of the chorus ; its second
reappearance takes place just after Zurga's " *Si tu
reste fidèle*," as the priestess recognises Nadir ;
its third comes towards the end of the act, when
Nadir calls upon his loved one's name ; and in
the third act the composer summons it to his aid,
at the point where Leïla approaches Zurga in
order to plead for Nadir.

In this opera Bizet did not throw his spear into
the future. The music owes much to the Italian
style ; it owes something (*e.g.* the melody which
occurs in the prelude) to Gounod, and, as was said
on its appearance, it may owe a little to Félicien
David. Within limits, it reveals a lively talent
and a competent musicianship. It does not
prove, however, that either talent or musicianship
was used with wise economy, or in deference to an
order or system, without which much of a musician's power will always waste itself in thin air.
Whatever he may have been later, Bizet at twenty-
six was not, as here seen, extremely critical of
himself. A number written, he evidently did not
look at it closely, and ask if it were the best he
could do. Technically, there is not much to be
said, but it would be unwise to leave unnoticed the
immoderate use of the diminished seventh, that

very pleasant help in time of operatic trouble, which is here abused quite as much as Wagner abused the tremolo in *The Flying Dutchman*.

La Jolie Fille de Perth is after Scott—a long way after Scott. Those who rise from a reading of the novel and go to hear the opera will not utter a word of protest at this statement, nor will they, if seasoned opera-goers, be much surprised by the discovery. Plays and novels, when turned into operas, have a way of changing their natures. The better they are as plays and novels, the more they change. The merit of a play or novel lies in plot, word, and characterisation ; and, in the case of many novels, there is the added merit of fine description. Opera may not always seriously affect the plot ; it generally makes woeful havoc of words and characterisation, and it cannot, however good it be, provide any equivalent for inspired descriptive writing. The change undergone by a play or novel when it is transformed into an opera, a change of which even the most superficial hearer must be conscious, can, therefore, readily be explained. A vast quantity of the material that is not only necessary, but fruitful, to playwright or novelist assumes a very different aspect when it comes to be dealt with by librettist and composer. Much conversation will have to be thrown overboard quite mercilessly, as it will not bear association with music. The landscapes traced so lovingly by the prose writer must be scored through with a blue pencil.

Emotional and lyrical elements are brought into a new prominence. And, partly as a result of this proceeding, partly as a result of the presence of music, the characters come to us in fresh guise. They may answer to their names, yet we know full well that they have, like Lewis Carroll's Alice, stepped suddenly into another world. Change is in the nature of the case inevitable ; and we must, if we are to enjoy opera at all, permit a wide latitude. Nevertheless, there are limits, to exceed which is to incur censure. We are within our right when we ask that the operatic version of a theme shall be in all things as faithful to the original as circumstances permit. When it wanders far from the original, the opera-makers would do well to adopt a fresh title.

The statement that *La Jolie Fille de Perth* is based on Scott must be taken to mean that the initial impulse came from the romancer's pages : it means little, if anything, more. The choice of the subject was, indeed, curious and likely to involve the framers of the plot in more than a few nasty problems, which it would have taken a great deal of resource and adroitness to solve. The book itself was, as Lockhart said, " highly popular", if never classed with Scott's performances of " the first file". It will be best appreciated by Scotsmen, for whom the incidents and the descriptions of familiar spots will always possess more attraction than they can ever possess for the " foreigner". It is essentially local and introduces types seldom understood, but often misrepresented abroad. For no country, I think, suffers more from ridiculous travesties of the life, manners, sentiments, and habits of its natives than Scotland, which even to-day is often interpreted to the world by music-hall comedians, and made to yield material for money, whisky, and kirk jests by people who are ignorant of their ignorance. But, were we cynically minded, we might take a perverse joy in seeing the opera as it is ; for the Balzac of *Maître Cornélius* complained that in *Quentin Durward* Scott, through a " singular caprice", placed Plessis-les-Tours upon a height, whereas it stood in a hollow. Figuratively speaking, Plessis-les-Tours has often been upon a height, and it is most assuredly upon a height here. Or, to put it otherwise, this opera is not *a Fair Maid of Perth* at all, but *a Fair Maid of Operadom*, or *a Fair Maid of Romance*. Pigot, then, is not far wrong when he suggests that the lady in question has emerged into her new environment as " *La Jolie Gantière d'ou vous voudrez*". The old ballad has it that " Bonny St. Johnston stands on Tay " ; what is supposed to be bonny St. Johnston here stands most prominently on Seine. To be sure, the whole is seen through French spectacles. It was by the merest chance, one feels, that the Wizard of the North was drawn upon, and, once drawn upon, there was no very serious effort to give the opera the spirit or atmosphere of the original. Surely, the plot was

simply a plot, and so much material out of which
an operatic garment might be cut in the way
operatic garments generally are cut. The work
is an attempt to carry a certain kind of romance
into alien territory that befits it not. The sky
above is a French sky ; the figures bear themselves as French men and women do ; and when
they open their mouths they proclaim the real
country of their origin—which is not Scotland.
La Jolie Fille de Perth is no more Scots than
Fidelio is Spanish. If Bizet were a commercial
traveller in music, he did not carry about with him
a sample of Scots homespun.

The opera was written speedily, very probably
too speedily, and in glancing at it one ought to
remember that the composer was not enamoured
of the novel. "*A propos* of the novel of Walter
Scott, I ought to avow my heresy. I find it
detestable. It is a detestable novel, but it is an
excellent book", he told Galabert, who details the
numbers which Bizet most admired—the duet
for Catherine and Henry in the first act ; the
ronde de nuit chorus, the *danse bohémienne* and
Ralph's solo in the second act ; the duet between
Mab and the Duke, with its music " off " in the
third act ; and in the fourth the opening number
and the St Valentine chorus.

While the opera may be, and has been, listened
to with pleasure, it would be absurd to shut one's
eyes to its obvious defects. It lacks that one
unmistakable, conquering touch, which tells us

that a musical intelligence had concentrated terrifically upon its task ; the one unmistakable, conquering touch, compared with which other qualities are as nought. We can say all that really need be said of the score without resorting to the word inevitable. We never feel that Bizet had rejected one hundred things in order to arrive at the better, or best, one hundred and first. There is much, very much, in it that would come readily to the mind of a musician, but should have been hammered diligently on the anvil of his thought. This applies to the opening forge chorus and to the St Valentine chorus ; it applies also to the drinking song, which celebrates the glories of Spanish and French wines, where I think the composer has not made the most of his chances. My impression, and I give it for what it may be worth, is that Bizet relied over much on his craftsmanship, and too little on his better self. The formulae, the routine methods, of the opera composer are too frequently in evidence.

But, in justice, it must be said that there are pages that stand out above the rest. The couplets of Mab have the lightness Bizet so often courted successfully. The *danse bohémienne*, which has been likened to a dervish chorus in the *Ruins of Athens*, is Bizet nearly, if not quite, at his best. The duet for Mab and the Duke, with its distant instrumental background, has a pleasing charm and a tranquil atmosphere. There is a theme of romantic warmth, and, parenthetically, a phrase in the finale of Act III, which is vividly recalled by Sir Walford Davies's " Solemn Melody". As for prophecy or promise, it is not overstepping the mark to say that the last few bars of the duet for Catherine and Henry in Act I, from " *Oui, cette fleur* " to the end, hint at the not dissimilar termination of the duet for Micaela and Don José, which occurs towards the beginning of *Carmen*. Nor would one be far out in declaring that the quartet of the first act seems a kind of early and rough sketch of the ensemble, " *Quant au douanier*", which figures in the mountain scene of the later work ; though there is, of course, a marked difference. The weakness of the earlier number, as has been pointed out, lies in the somewhat unsatisfactory treatment accorded to the words sung by Mab, Henry and the Duke. No sound defence can be put forward for such a thing as the Duke's " *Ah ! ah ! la rencontre est imprévue, Une femme ?* " and so on ; for " *im* " (staccato) is separated "*-prévue* (also staccato) by two beats filled by rests, and " *une*", which falls on the fourth and first beats, is similarly separated from " *femme* ". This is uncommonly like the line of least resistance, and has, of course, no exact counterpart in the *Carmen* excerpt. There, it is true, the tenors and basses sing staccato, but, as the notes fall on every beat, no outrage is perpetrated on the words.

If *La Jolie Fille de Perth* marks an advance on its predecessor, the extent of the advance cannot

be called very great. In neither work does
Bizet sound an exceedingly original note. In
neither does he appear to have found something
sufficiently inspiring to move him to the very
depths of his being. If he did, one has resignedly
to admit either that the reward somehow escaped
him, or that his artistic personality had not yet
gained its fulness of strength. I cannot help
asking myself if he really gave the best of which he
was capable in these two operas ; if, in an ivory
tower, thinking of his theme, minding not a whit
the views of a world that has always been " demned
censorious ", he could not at this stage of his
career have made more of his subjects, far from
perfect as they are. No doubt, in a real sense
the writing and production of the operas were not
idle tasks ; no doubt, the time spent upon their
composition taught him many things. One can
hardly believe that so practical a man as Bizet did
not learn the lesson which experience, and that
alone, can give to the dramatic composer. After
La Jolie Fille de Perth, Bizet wrote that the school
of flonflons and roulades was dead, which certainly
seems to imply that for the future he would not
keep his ear so close upon the ground. Apart
from this, it is possible that, in some quiet moment,
he took stock of his position and asked himself
whether really, truly, and with singleness of
purpose he had set out upon the exciting search
for his ego.

Djamileh, at any rate, is a performance far

superior to the twin productions of the 'sixties. Four years separated *La Jolie Fille de Perth* from *Les Pêcheurs de Perles*. Five years separated *Djamileh* from *La Jolie Fille de Perth*. But it is necessary to be on guard against the deceptiveness of mere dates. Looked at in the light of art and general accomplishment, *Djamileh* is more widely removed from *La Jolie Fille de Perth* than a study of the calendar would suggest. As we saw, many things happened to the composer between 1867 and 1872, and it may safely be added that the man who wrote *Djamileh* had travelled along the road of development very much farther than the composer of the previous decade.

At first Bizet was not exceptionally fortunate in the plots which were set down upon his writing-desk by poets and managers. One cannot help speculating as to how far the success of *Carmen* is due to the fact that in this particular case he had to work with a good *intrigue*, the prevailing temperature, the passion, and the overflowing emotion of which recommended themselves to his artistic and sun-loving nature. The uniqueness of *Carmen* might, in part, be traced to the meeting of *the* man and *the* work, and to the natural corollary that the man was " in " the work from the start. Such reflections will spring, sooner or later, from a scrutiny of *Djamileh*, which no one will feel called upon to reproach with theatricality. It is possible to exaggerate the merits of movement and incident, though there seems

little chance of their being exaggerated at a time
when movement is so often considered vulgar and
incident childish ; it is possible to turn opera into
a glorified Lord Mayor's show, just as it is possible
to turn it into a mannequin parade, or an exhibition of pseudo-antique furniture, as it is possible
to do a hundred things, wise and absurd, with it.
Do what you will, I say, but whatever you do,
always keep in mind that opera is to be played in
the theatre.   Once that great central fact is
forgotten everything is lost.   You have courted
the failure which has come upon your head.   A
plague on those who carry opera into the regions
of arid philosophy.   An opera must be theatrical,
though in saying so one does not accept the
unfortunate connotation of the word.

The trouble with *Djamileh* is one that afflicts
all slender works and will be felt by composer,
interpreters and audience alike.   Where the
material is of so fragile a kind the composer stands
between Scylla and Charybdis.   If he does not
aid it he stands reproached ; if he takes too much
out of it he is guilty of false valuation of its
potentialities.   How much Bizet made of the
libretto put into his hands will be recognised if
the story be told in a few words.

Djamileh, or *L'Esclave Amoureuse* is based on de
Musset's *Namouna*.   The action passes in Cairo,
the Cairo so well loved by story-tellers, a city of
picturesque vistas and high colours, in which the
impossible may happen at any hour of the day.

The period is best indicated by the convenient word, mediæval. A young prince, Haroun by name, lives a life of ease and plenty. So richly blessed with this world's goods is he that he need deny himself nothing ; his slightest desire is satisfied as if by magic, his passing whims are humoured by a hundred eager satellites. In spite of this, or rather because of it, Haroun finds life is empty, dull, and bereft of meaning, as the rich and idle young man of every age has found it. With the most coveted treasures at his elbow, with all the luxury and bounty of the East at his beck and call, he wears a rueful countenance, and is restless, fretful and dissatisfied. Philosophers would soon have told him what was wrong. Haroun ought to have engaged in some honest work and lived on his modest wages—but then, there would have been no opera. Djamileh, a beautiful slave (operatic slaves are invariably beautiful) is in love with this blasé and distracted young aristocrat. Her love is unrequited by him, but Splendiano, his factotum, is enamoured of her. Djamileh, tender and clinging creature though she be, is determined to conquer. To this end she disguises herself, and joins a troupe of slaves which a slave-dealer brings to Haroun. She dances before him, and he decides to buy her. When he penetrates her disguise she confesses her true love. For a moment Haroun hesitates, then with resolution he tells her that she has vainly returned. Djamileh pleads in broken voice ; her

love is all she has. She bids him adieu for ever and
ever, and prepares to depart. Haroun, strangely
converted, if that be the correct term, runs after
her, throws his arms around her, and sings her
praises in ecstatic fashion. A love duet follows.
At the end of the opera, Splendiano appears, and,
seeing that his chances have disappeared, throws
up his hands in despair. We are left wondering
how long the peevish young gentleman and the
faithful Djamileh will enjoy domestic bliss.

The dramatic scheme is, therefore, of the
simplest ; on the one hand, the bored and rich
Haroun ; on the other, the affectionate and poor
Djamileh, while, standing between them, we behold the comic figure of Splendiano. It is not
hard to lay a finger on the weakest spot of the
book. We have learned much of Haroun. We
know his nature. One does not need to be a
detective to see that he is, for all his grandeur, a
spoiled child, who, like every spoiled child,
quickly tires of the most amusing toys. He does
not know what he wants, or, to be precise, he does
not know that happiness has little to do with
material possessions. In view of this, it might
seem that his passionate repulse of Djamileh and
his equally passionate reception of her, which
follows so speedily, have an air of psychological
truth. One might even contend that such a
changeable individual is just the individual to
protest his affection in the most extravagant
terms. Again, one might contend that the

sudden surrender is out of key with Haroun's antecedents. But the weakness, in my view, lies not so much in the change as in the way it is brought about. Only twenty odd bars separate Haroun's " *va-t'en !* " from his apostrophe to Djamileh's beauty and devotion. Admittedly, one has to make concessions. As operas are not written for Chinamen who are boys when the curtain goes up and aged mandarins when it falls, a telescoping of incidents is inevitable ; and the telescoping process is likely to be more drastic in the case of one-act operas than in those of greater length. But the telescoping has been overdone here. The incident is the pivot of the opera, after which we have only a romantic love duet which rounds off the piece innocuously. I think it should not have been beyond the wit of man to make more of Haroun's dismissal of Djamileh, his struggle against himself, and his surrender to her charms.

Taken as a whole, the book is anti-theatrical. In spite of highbrows, the child-like in man yearns for some sort of happening on the stage. This being so, nothing is more likely to bore a normal audience than a theatrical piece suffering either from paralysis or pernicious anaemia. As will be gathered, not very much happens on the stage in the course of *Djamileh*, and what happens is far from world-shaking. No plot could, in fact, have been less likely to tickle the none too sensitive palate of a post-war public. Bizet realised

the inherent weakness of the book. I imagine
that he lamented the absence of something with a
larger human interest and a wider appeal, but, be
it remembered, he was satisfied with his music
which now demands attention.

In speaking of the score it is only right to bear
in mind that Bizet was threatened with danger
from three quarters when he set *Djamileh*. He
had to deal with an oriental subject, and oriental
subjects always have their pitfalls ; he had to
deal with a weak libretto ; and, finally, he had to
deal with the problems inseparable from the
writing of a one-act piece.

The hearer will first be struck by the fact that
the composer has made real progress in the gaining of a mastery over himself. The moments
that make us feel he had chosen the easy road are
fewer than those of the earlier operas. The ideas
with which he works have the appearance of a
greater spontaneity ; the way in which he handles
them shows a distinct improvement. He uses a
more pointed pen. There is a neatness and crisp-
ness that he carries off with an airy grace. Even
if the reader be disinclined to endorse Pigot, who,
while calling the opera an error from the scenic
point of view, describes it as " a little masterpiece,
a pearl, a jewel " ; even if he think that Marmontel's eulogy of it as "a charming, dreamy,
passionate work full of the oriental languor that
Félicien David and Reyer have so happily caught
in their delicious scores, *Lalla Roukh* and *La*

Statue " errs by its excessive enthusiasm, he will be likely to accord it a higher position than anything Bizet had before accomplished. To do so is but to deal out justice.

The opening is effective. Haroun reclines smoking, Splendiano sits at a low table, writing. From afar off come the voices of the chorus, singing a song of sundown. To the sopranos are given the melody and the words ; to the rest of the choristers vague and mysterious chords, sung with closed lips. A persistent tambourine marks the rhythm. Haroun raises his voice lazily and tells of the visions that pass before him in his idle reverie. A phrase of breadth and comely grace announces the approach of Djamileh, who passes across the scene and throws a look of tenderness at Haroun. This is one of the best moments in the work. The indolent strains heard at the opening return, and give way to a lively duet for Haroun and Splendiano, the music of which fits the mood like a glove. There is no depth, but depth is not required. Haroun's interpolated " *Tu veux savoir* "—the profession of faith of an epicure, Pigot calls it—possesses a melodic charm that culminates in the refrain. Djamileh returns and tells of a dream she has had. The slight shadow which has meanwhile overshadowed the score dissipates when Splendiano, followed by slaves, busies himself with supper, the last supper Djamileh shall partake of in Haroun's house. At this point, the music prattles along delightfully.

Djamileh then sings, at Haroun's request, accompanying herself on the lute. Her plaintive song, called by Bizet a ghazel, recounts how a simple maiden loved Nour-Eddin, King of Lahore. Haroun who, Omar Khayyam-like, loves mirth and laughter, does not appreciate it. His friends arrive and greet him in lusty chorus. The haunting tune to which the words, " *Quelle est cette belle* " are set must be marked down as truly Bizet-like, and ought to be compared with the song *Le Gascon*, to which it bears a close affinity. The next number is a short chanson, " *La fortune est femme*," trolled in the distance by Haroun and his companions. Then comes Djamileh's lament, a page of doubt and apprehension. The slaves arrive to the sound of the curiously harsh and piquant march subject, which does duty in the overture. This subject in its precision, rhythm, and piquancy is characteristic of the author. Surrounded by Haroun's friends, the slaves execute their steps. A leggiero and staccato love ditty for Splendiano stands between the almée dance and the final duet. Grace and simplicity abound in it. The duet itself is much better at the opening than at the finish. At the opening it flows along naturally. As Haroun proclaims his philosophy to her whom he takes for the new slave, Bizet returns to the theme used when the epicurean pooh-poohed the sad accents of the ghazel ; and as Djamileh determines to disclose her identity she sings again the sad melody of that sorrowful number. All this is well managed and effective. With the throwing aside of all pretence, the story of the opera is at an end, but the maker of the book must have thought that something in the way of a rounding-off was called for, and, fearful of a Manx-cat termination, he provided a love duet. From this point the value of the music declines. One is reminded of Gounod, and of Gounod not at his best.

The exotic note is to be found in the opening chorus, in the ghazel and in the almée dance, where Bizet evoked the orient, which he did not know at first hand. I am not in a position to endorse Reyer's remark that this is " the true music of the east." The composer wished to give his opera the measure of local colour necessary in order to proclaim its *locale*. I do not imagine that he troubled about the scientific aspect of the matter, nor do I imagine that one should regret this. His East is, if you will, the East of imaginative convention, as Balzac's Italy is the Italy of imaginative convention. How it would strike an oriental I know not, for Bizet, so far as I am aware, relied entirely upon his own judgment and drew solely upon his imagination. Many other composers have done the same, and with varying results. The Eastern portions of *Djamileh* are not likely to be submitted to the scientific test except by scientifically-minded people, of whom there are few in the average audience. It may, therefore, be said that the writer attained what he set out to do ; he has imparted a flavour to some parts of the opera in a manner not likely to be anything save acceptable to the hearer. If the objection be raised that *Djamileh* is spasmodically Eastern—what is there of the East in the final duet ?—let it be conceded that this is true. Let it be conceded also that the opera which is Eastern, wholly Eastern, and nothing but Eastern, has yet to be written. There are exotic pages in *Aïda* and in *Madame Butterfly*. Verdi and Puccini desired to remind us that the scenes of action are Egypt and Japan respectively. To this end they introduced music that is extra-European, but they could do so only spasmodically. When their music ceases to be music of colour and decoration, when it becomes lyrical, the extra-European note is to seek. So is it with *Djamileh*. Bizet has recognised the limitations which the writer of an Eastern opera must recognise. He may not have allowed himself all the rein he could have taken without disaster. It must, nevertheless, be granted that the occasional appearance of the Eastern note cannot be set down as a mark against him. To compose an opera entirely Eastern in its music is impossible ; were it possible, I should not care to guarantee its general acceptance.

Of the libretto and the plot Bizet made good use. Neither helped him very much. His music is rather charming than powerful, and it is not dull. That for this slender story and not very inspiring book he performed so adequate a service says something for his resources and his gift for pleasing. One wonders how *Djamileh* would have stood had there been no *Carmen* ; one wonders whether the shadow of *Carmen* has, in part, obscured this delicate flower, or whether the fame of *Carmen* is responsible for a more generous critical appreciation of its predecessor than would have been the case had *Djamileh* been the last dramatic work. Looked at by itself, the piece may be credited with much pleasing music of a light kind, with a considerable amount of taking melody, and with several effective strokes ; in view of which it earns a meritorious place in the ranks of one-act operas.

After an interval of three years came *Carmen*, one of the most popular operas in the wide world, and one which thoroughly deserves every atom of the popularity that it has enjoyed. The source of the plot was found in Mérimée's tale of the same name, which belongs to 1845, and had by 1875 become something of a classic. Concerning this literary masterpiece, I cannot do better than quote the words of Mr. Saintsbury, who, in his valuable *History of the French Novel*, writes :

" Of the unfaulty faultlessness of that original there has never been any denial worth listening to ; the gainsayers having been persons who succumbed either to non-literary prejudice of one kind or another or the peculiarly childish habit of going against established opinion. For combined interest of matter and perfection of form I should put it among the best dozen short stories of the world so far as I am acquainted with them. . . . From the story itself not a word could be abstracted without loss nor one added to it without danger."

It is possible to talk of Mérimée's *Carmen* and the operatic *Carmen*, and to mark the existing differences. No sensible person will hold up his hands in horror when he discovers that the opera is in some respects unlike the book. A comparison is illuminating, because it shows how much of the original was carried to the libretto and the stage, and how much of it left out of the reckoning. The chief differences may briefly be stated. Of necessity, a good deal that goes to Mérimée's tale the perfect thing it is has been discarded. The entire Gibraltar episode has been abandoned, and Garcia le Borgne is left in the lurch. Lucas, the picador of the story, yields to rebaptising and treads the boards as Escamillo, the espada. With this change of name and status, he becomes a more important personage in his relation to the plot. Micaela, the blond Navarese, on the other hand, who does not appear in Mérimée at all, was invented by Meilhac and Halévy, obviously as the result of a search for a foil to Carmen. They probably took their cue from some words put into the mouth of Don José, when he speaks of the blue skirts and long plaits of hair that distinguished his countrywomen. Carmen herself becomes reincarnated, though, in saying so, one should be careful to make it plain that a reincarnation of some kind was inevitable. To carry the *Carmen* of Mérimée to the stage of the Opéra Comique was beyond human power. One must, consequently, distinguish between the changes wrought by transference to another medium of expression, and the changes, if any, for which the librettists are directly responsible.

Leaving the book and coming to the opera one is, certainly, very conscious of change. A great deal of the gloom, the roughness, the raggedness, and what generally may be termed the savage brutality of the story does not find a place there. This may be, to some extent, be attributed to music's tendency to throw a glamour over its subject. Clothed in melody, the unromantic often becomes romantic, and the unlovely garbs itself in the mantle of poetry. But it would be unwise to forget that the opera is " *tiré de la nouvelle de Prosper Mérimée*," and that the singers have it in their power, if they are gifted with imagination and a taste for getting at the heart of a matter, to carry something of the atmosphere and wildness of the book with them. This is particularly true of Carmen. In order to get under the skin of the cigarette girl, Calvé went to Seville and mixed with the Spanish factory workers. While all singers are not able to do this, they can consult the story, and would do themselves and their public excellent service by reading, marking, and inwardly digesting it. The opera offers plenty of scope for imaginative talent ; in none other that I can think of is there less excuse for prosaic and merely routine work, and the very fact that the stage piece is based on Mérimée should quickly send the executant to his pages. My point is merely this ; that the singer ought not to neglect the author ; that he, or she, has it in his, or her, power to build up an interpretation upon a foundation provided by Mérimée. It seems to me that this is more than a choice ; it is a duty.

With this in mind, one is the more astonished at the reproach hurled at Galli-Marié for being too realistic. Whatever she did, the singer stood to be censured. If she sought the key to *Carmen's* character in Mérimée's pages she was too frank and vulgar ; she portrayed the novelist's, not the librettists', Carmen. If she played the part without thinking of Mérimée at all, she portrayed Meilhac and Halévy's Carmen, not Mérimée's. I need hardly say that there exist three possible Carmens : Mérimée's, Meilhac and Halévy's, and the singer's, and that the last named will not, in all cases, be exactly the same as either the first or the second. I myself cannot clearly see how the stage Carmen could have been made very different from what she is. In extracting a figure from the printed page and placing it upon the stage something is lost, something altered, and something gained. The loss, the alteration and the gain, the nature, as well as the extent, of the loss, alteration and gain will

depend largely upon the skill and conscience of
the individual involved in the delicate transaction ;
in other words, upon the skill and conscience of
the librettist. As they sit in the theatre, people
who are keenly alive to the literary qualities of
Mérimée will miss many of the good things to
be found in the story. Mr. Saintsbury tells us
as much when, in the work already quoted, he
writes :

> " All the world knows *Carmen,* though it may be feared that
> the knowledge has been conveyed to more people by the
> mixed and inferior medium of the stage and music than by
> the pure literature of the original tale. Yet it may be gener-
> ously granted that the lower introduction may have induced
> some to go on, or back, to the higher."

Of course, the controversy centres mainly in
Carmen herself. More than once it has been
asserted that Carmen lost something which really
and truly belonged to her when she stepped
through the stage-door to enter the realms of
song. The habits and deportment of a Spanish
gypsy mingle with those of a Parisian street-girl.
She has discarded something of the wildness of
the sierras to assume something of the French
manner. If this be strictly true, though I fear
the prima-donna has it in her power to emphasise
or keep in check the Parisian note, the explanation
may be found in the uniqueness of Mérimée's
experience and talents. He had travelled in
Spain, and owned to finding himself at home only
with unpretentious people whom he had long

known, and in a Spanish *venta* with muleteers and
peasant women of Andalusia. He sought to
paint a picture of a Romany *chi*, alive in every
fibre of her being. The aim of the librettists was
not identical. The business of Meilhac and
Halévy was to take from the book what they
considered useful for their purpose, and leave the
rest. How far they succeeded in this task may
be left to the reader to decide. For my part, I
think they made a good showing. I am perfectly
willing, here as elsewhere, to recognise generously
the difficulties with which the adapter is called
upon to struggle, and I observe that the opera
Carmen is in the fortunate condition of possessing
an admirable plot which, with some modification,
might conceivably hold the attention of an audience without music. As much cannot be said
of many operas.

Sifting this question of *Carmen* the tale and
Carmen the opera, of Carmen the gypsy of Mérimée, and Carmen the chief character of the opera,
one must bear in mind that several hands were
at work ; Mérimée the originator, Meilhac and
Halévy the librettists, Bizet the composer. In
the case of Carmen there is also the exponent to
be reckoned with. One must bear in mind,
further, that there are inevitable and gratuitous
changes in the making of an opera from a story.
Ultimately, loving Mérimée's tale as we are
bound to do, we may well rejoice that a veritable
masterpiece of literature inspired a veritable

masterpiece of dramatic art. Recollecting the
destruction wrought by some of those who have
laid Vandal hands upon literary and dramatic
productions and outraged our respect for the
amenities, that is something for which to be de-
voutly thankful. The operatic Carmen is not
exactly the Carmen of word and page ; it could
not be. Taking the story on the one hand, and
the opera on the other, mercilessly subjecting the
latter to the most acid of tests, remembering the
exigencies and limitations of the theatre, remembering the conditions imposed by the presence of
music, we cannot say that the operatic version
does grave injustice to the original. This has
disappeared, that has been introduced, the mar-
shalling of incidents has been altered. We shall
deplore, while we admit its inevitability, a loss on
the literary side. We are yet left with a human
story, a story palpitating with life, whose characters live, and move, and have their being.

The dramatic scheme designed by Meilhac and
Halévy is well known. As the curtain rises we
see a square in Seville. To the right stands a
cigarette factory, to the left a guard-house. People
are coming and going, and a group of soldiers
catches the eye. Micaela approaches timidly
with a questioning look. Morales, the officer on
duty, asks her whom she seeks. It is one called
José, who will not appear until the guard is
changed. No matter. Carried away by her
naïve charm, Morales and the soldiers endeavour

to persuade the bashful girl to remain with them for the present, but, with a promise to return, she runs off quickly. Preceded by a number of street lads, the change of guard now arrives with two officers, Zuniga, a captain, and José, a corporal. Morales tells José of the frightened visitor who sought him. "It must have been Micaela," exclaims the corporal. Zuniga twits him about the fair, blue-eyed young maiden who has made him suddenly so pensive, whereat he confesses his affection for her. The dialogue is interrupted by the factory bell calling the girls to work. They begin to pass across the square, smiling to the young men who await the procession, and in friendly groups enter the factory door. But one, and that not the least fascinating, has not yet turned up. Hardly have some members of the crowd commented upon Carmen's absence than she appears. In a moment she forms the centre of attraction. The men surround her, and vow themselves her slaves. When will she repay their love ? Haughtily she replies that she does not know ; perhaps to-morrow, not to-day. The habanera, as true an index of her character as " *La donna e mobile* " is of that of the Duke in *Rigoletto*, follows. In the singing she has caught sight of José, who, sitting astride a chair, works at a broken chain, thinking the while of Micaela. Of course, he takes no notice of Carmen, in spite of her attempt to divert his attention. Throwing a flower to him with a disdainful laugh, she turns on her heels and rushes into the factory. José is for an instant stunned. The flower makes him feel as if he had been shot. He picks it up and looks at it—it is beautiful ; he smells it—the perfume is delicious ; it reminds him of the giver —ah, the witch ! He places the blossom in his tunic.

He has just made this first surrender when Micaela comes back. Her presence is particularly welcome, as it helps to chase away thoughts of the dangerous siren, and as she brings a message from home which awakens sweet memories of his native village and the happy days of boyhood. Micaela leaves him to read this message, and José, thinking of his mother and Micaela, laughs at Carmen's endeavours to throw her spell over him. Great commotion among the cigarette girls interrupts his reflections. A quarrel between two of them has resulted in the wounding of one of the disputants, and Carmen is denounced as the culprit. She is arrested. Zuniga asks her for an explanation. Carmen, who has not the slightest intention of tamely submitting to discipline, promptly proceeds to make a fool of the officer. Threatening her with prison, he leaves her in charge of José. This gives the girl her chance. She sings of a soldier she adores— a song that has the desired effect, for José is carried away and declares his love. Throwing restraints to the winds and unmindful of his duty, he frees her hands, which have been tied behind her back, leaving the rope in them, however, to make it seem as though they were still bound. Zuniga returns with an order for her imprisonment and commands José to escort her to her quarters. Scarcely have the pair set out than Carmen throws the rope into the midst of the throng, which has meantime collected in the square, and in the general confusion disappears.

The second scene is the inn of Lillas Pastia, where we discover a motley crew, including Carmen and Zuniga, officers and gypsies. After some dancing a cry goes up. Escamillo, the toreador, is coming. He enters, is acclaimed, sings his famous song, and pays homage to Carmen, who receives him coldly. He departs and, the hour being late, Lillas Pastia closes the door. The smugglers Remendado and Dancairo, appear. They suggest that Carmen should induce José to join their band. As they creep away, José arrives. For him the siren dances a bewitching dance into which she infuses all her devilry. When a bugle sounds the call to barracks, José makes a movement as if to obey. Carmen pours out on him the vials of her wrath and upbraids him with the cooling of his love. He shows how false this is by drawing forth the flower she had thrown at him and uttering the passionate accents of the flower song. Carmen continues to upbraid him. If he loved her, he would follow her to the mountains. José, who has still a little of the soldier left in him, knows what that would mean. At this moment of crisis, Zuniga bursts open the door. The two men fly at one another, only to be separated by the smugglers, whom Carmen hastily summons. José has lifted his hand against his superior—another step towards his degradation. He is now willing to follow the she-devil to the gypsies' lair.

The next scene reveals a rocky place among the mountains. José is still tortured by shame. He thinks of his mother, who imagines that her son lives the life of an honest soldier. Carmen jeers at his dejection in her insolent way, bidding him leave, as a smuggler's life is not for him. This would mean separation, a thing not to be contemplated. "Perhaps," says Carmen, "you would kill me?" She cares not, for, after all, Destiny settles everything. The girls, Frasquita and Mercedes, proceed to see what the future holds for them by means of cards, and in bantering manner recite the good fortune they are to have— a youthful lover who becomes a great soldier, in the one case, a rich old man who gives his wife jewels and considerately expires, in the other. Carmen, too, consults the cards; she turns up spades—death! The company of smugglers moves on, leaving José to guard the rear. Shortly after, Micaela, timid and appealing as ever, ventures upon the scene, having been led to this haunt. José is upon a neighbouring rock and Micaela hesitates to join him there, when he takes aim and fires at an approaching figure, that of Escamillo, whom he nearly kills. After an interchange of words, none too cordial, the couple get to grips. Their scuffling attracts some of the smugglers, not yet afar off; they separate the fighters. Carmen has not forgotten the handsome toreador, who then and there invites the company to the approaching bull-fight at Seville. One of the smugglers spies Micaela hiding in the vicinity. She is brought into the midst of the crowd. José's mother is dying and longs to see him. Carmen tells him he had better go, which utterance only intensifies his jealousy. He agrees, however, to follow Micaela, not without warning Carmen, in threatening words, that he will meet her again. The crowd moves off, and Escamillo's voice is heard singing the refrain of the toreador's song. Carmen listens to it enraptured, while José, led by Micaela, prepares to descend the mountain.

With the fourth act we are again in a square of Seville, at the back of which stands the entrance to the bull-ring. The street crowd is moving about, highly excited at the prospect of a good day's sport. As the celebrities of the ring pass along, the people acclaim them in vigorous and enthusiastic fashion. Escamillo comes last of all, to the bravos of his admirers. Carmen, beaming with pleasure, is by his side. Before going to prepare for the fray, he tells her of his love in a tender passage. Carmen remains in the square awaiting the smugglers. Frasquita and

Mercedes take this opportunity of warning her against José, who has been seen mixing with the throng ; but if they think Carmen will take precautions, they have not read her character aright. Whatever she is, she is not a coward. She determines to remain in the square and meet her enemy if need be.

José, demented and dishevelled, and a ghost of his former self, creeps up to her. He coaxes her. Let her only forget the past and flee with him to some foreign part. Carmen unromantically informs him that all is over. José persists in his entreaties, but without success. " I love you no more," she says, after reminding him that Carmen disdains to tell a lie. Again he entreats her, protests his devotion, and implores her not to leave him. Carmen brushes him aside. She was born free, and free she means to die. Inside the building the crowd shouts *vivas* at Escamillo, the man for whom this woman has deserted José. Carmen wishes to witness his triumph, but José, now desperate, threatens her with a knife. Fearlessly, she proclaims her love for the popular favourite. Again come shouts from the multitude, roused to enthusiastic admiration by Escamillo's exploits with the bull. Carmen tries once more to pass into the bull-ring, struggling awhile with the man she has made mad. A brief and final appeal comes from his lips. Carmen boldly challenges him to stab her at once. Yet again a shout of victory. She rushes for the entrance and is about to pass through the door when José follows her, seizes her, and plunges his knife into her back. At this moment, the air is filled with voices announcing the success of the toreador. The people begin to rush out into the square, horrified to find what has happened. José, limp and distraught, gives himself up to the soldiers.

Whether one has a taste for this kind of plot or not, and there will be many varieties of opinion, it cannot be denied that the one under discussion provides excellent dramatic material. Bizet had been not too lucky in the plots for which he had previously provided music, and it almost seems as if the fates had conspired to offer generous compensation in the shape of *Carmen*. A cheerful acknowledgment that not anything like the whole of Mérimée appears can cheerfully be made, because there remain so much to grip the attention of the hearer. If dullness be, as I think it is, a great artistic vice, the absence of dullness must be accounted a great artistic virtue. How the fifty-year-old *Carmen* strikes young Chelsea I know not ; how it strikes those who are constitutionally incapable of enjoying opera is to me the darkest of secrets. This I do know ; that I find in it no dullness at all. The interest which it has for me, and I suppose for many others since it remains so popular, springs from several sources. For one thing, something definite happens in each act. To mark this down as a good feature is, no doubt, to lay oneself open to a charge of naïveté. When nothing happens it is always possible to blame the gainsayer for his lack of subtlety, a proceeding which invariably adds to your own reputation for unusual penetration. In this opera something *does* happen ; but not something which, if you fail to grasp a thin thread held out to you, is, to use an expressive phrase of Mr. Chesterton, " a mass of clotted nonsense." In the first act we behold Don José's earliest departure from the strict path of duty, which renders Carmen's escape possible. In the second, we behold his further departure from that path in his crossing swords with an officer, and in his throwing respectability to the winds by deciding to join the smugglers. In the third, for all his surrenders, he is further from happiness than ever, and tortured by the thought that, while he returns home, Carmen will be enjoying herself with his rival. The fourth, bringing us the inevitable outcome, discloses the man reduced to the lowest state.

There is incident and movement, then, in plenty. Nor is this all. The chief characters, though Carmen dominates them, are creatures of flesh and blood. They move amid picturesque surroundings. The eye feasts upon two bright and sunny scenes, and even Lillas Pastia's tavern is lent a dash of exotic colour by reason of the presence of the gypsies and the officers. We are in Spain, that strong-box which holds its ancient secrets so jealously ; in Spain, the country of smugglers, beggars, soldiers and gypsies ; in

Spain where the sun shines and the dagger is a potent argument. And what if this be really an operatic Spain such as never existed ? Is the maker of operas to be denied a licence when we allow one' freely to the poet ? *Carmen* has been enormously popular. As I have said, it deserves this enormous popularity, which all enormously popular operas do not. We know that the term " music-drama " is usually applied to music-drama of the Wagnerian kind. Nevertheless, the restricted use of it has no real sanction. To works of more than one kind can the term be accurately applied. It applies quite faithfully to Verdi's *Otello* and to Moussorgsky's *Boris Godounov* ; it applies, I venture to think, to Bizet's *Carmen*. If drama expressed through music be the correct definition of a music-drama, it cannot very well be withheld from the work which stands at the head and front of all French operas, so far as they are known to me.

But it may be complained that this is a blood and thunder affair, that it deals with common people, raw passions, unwashed smugglers and a very questionable throng whose status and demeanour would certainly provide a novelty before Bruneau had put opera into dungarees. Carmen herself, needless to say, is a strong contrast to the usual run of pathetic, frail and innocent heroines, and is certainly a change from fashionable *poitrinaires*, faded Violettas, and the like. The lure which the character has for the singer-actress may, without danger, be attributed to the complexity of the same. Those who have studied the interpretations of the many famous Carmens must have observed how they differ from one another. Obviously, such a character may be read in more than one way. Carmen was savage, sensual, indolent, coquettish, superstitious and crafty. It is open to any singer to fix upon one of these traits, and give it emphasis. Calvé made a good point when she stressed the truth that Carmen was neither a liar nor a coward, and singers, whatever their reading of the part, must remember this. If they do, it is still open to them to express their own convictions while playing the gypsy. No one will call her an edifying person, but she is undoubtedly a good one from the dramatic and musical point of view, as her popularity with singers and public goes to show. I have spoken of the possible authentic interpretations, which brings to mind the disinclination of some singers to make Carmen as vulgar as she should be. Protest has sometimes been raised that this is a Parisian lady, nicely dressed and tastefully shod, whom one night in the sierras would have frightened out of her life. The charge is really made against the too refined, the too civilised dress and manner, rather than against the character *qua* character. Of all the Carmens I have seen, Maria Gay has been the most successful in suggesting the aspect of the woman which is commonly toned down by singers who wish to look pretty-pretty in their picturesque costumes, and tread the cobbled streets of Seville in the nicest little high-heeled shoes to be purchased in the Place Vendôme.[1]

Carmen dominates the opera ; there is no doubt as to that. Nevertheless, it would be too much to say that the remaining figures have no interest. Whether José is a negative sort of person or a person of individuality carried away on the flood of his own emotions, lies with the tenor. Exponents of José frequently present us with an entirely false portrait of the man at the very start. The story of the opera is the story of this man's gradual surrender to an overwhelming passion. The José of the last act must, consequently, be a very different man from the José of the first. Who is the man whom we set eyes on at the beginning ? A country fellow, unversed in the ways of the town, simple, trusting, unsophisticated, betraying at every step the awkwardness of the small provincial. When the men watched the girls go into the tobacco factory, the story tells us that José sat on his bench. He was a young fellow then, and did not believe in pretty girls who had not the blue skirts and plaits of hair to be seen in his own village. He was rather afraid of Andalusian women. At the first encounter with Carmen, when she made fun of of him, everybody began to laugh. Poor José

[1] It may be of interest to say that Mme. Göta Ljungberg's interpretation of Carmen caused some critical stir in Stockholm, and that through the press the singer gave her reasons for taking the line she did.

got red in the face, and could not find an answer.
The point of the first act, its full meaning, its
tragedy, if you like, lies in his meeting with the
subtle, daring, provocative gypsy, who has the
wit and gift for scheming that distinguish her
kind.   We see, or ought to see, that the innocent
and untested soldier is no fit adversary for her.
We should be made to feel the disparity in their
previous experience and in their mental equipment.
What we do often see is a José already a military
man about town, who may be relied upon to show
you the private entrance to the tavern round the
the corner.   What we often feel is that he knows
quite as much about the tactics and strategy of
love affairs as his *vis-à-vis* ; that they meet one
one another on an equal footing.   The impression
arises from an entirely erroneous conception of
the part.   It robs the first act of much of its
meaning, as it robs the *dénouement* of its fullness of
bitterness and poignancy.   At the finish we should
be moved by the change which has overtaken
José's fortunes.   We should be able to throw
our minds back to his early, honest, simple life,
his loyalty to his country, his idealisation of the
rustic beauty, Micaela, his deep affection for his
mother ;   and we should be able to contrast it
with his last desperate condition, an outcast con-
sumed by hate and revenge.   The truth of the
matter is that *Carmen* cannot be what it ought to
be if it is not considered first of all dramatically.
No work is further from the category which may

be designated as costume cantata. In its own way, I repeat, it is, for all the peculiarity of operatic nomenclature, a music-drama. It calls for acting, and good acting at that, as well as singing. The tenor who does not realise this or trouble to study the psychology of José has no earthly chance of getting inside his skin.[1]

So far as Escamillo is concerned, the main thing to be said is that he not only supplants José in Carmen's affections, but that he provides an antithesis to that unfortunate gentleman. When he first appears he is already a successful practitioner of his art. In the end, when José has fallen to the gutter, Escamillo wins yet another triumph. Operatically, the bull fighter is a hero in a sense in which most other sportsmen are not. Escamillo comes into the inn wearing upon his brow a halo of heroism and romance. He typifies the sunny land of Spain, " the land of mantillos and matadors," as it has been called. He is one of a band which counts for more than philosophers and politicians. He wears a scarlet stomacher, and is decked out in the traditional garb of the public's favourite. He is a ritualist, moving amidst a riot of colour and encouraged by a full-throated chorus. Some may find very little in this. They may find Escamillo a rather commonplace and vain man, devoted to a vulgar sport, whose right of entry

---

[1] Chaliapin has been credited with the remark that once in his life he regretted he was not a tenor—after his first reading of the *Carmen* score.

into the realms of opera may be questioned. I shall agree with them when I hear a good opera which has for one of its characters a cricketer or a baseball expert, or when Covent Gardens shows us a work in which the Oxford and Cambridge crews play a vital part. Ask yourself if W. G. Grace, Babe Ruth, or Capablanca belongs to the authentic world of opera as does Escamillo. Verily, romance lingers with us still.

Micaela was, as I suggested, introduced to provide a foil to Carmen. Except in the matter of truthfulness, she is everything that Carmen is not—timid, bashful, naïve, gentle and modest. She has been praised as a sweet and charming figure whose existence is due to a happy inspiration on the part of the librettists ; she has been dismissed as an insipid and peevish *ingénue* without whom there exists no *opéra-comique* worthy of the name. Of course, you may ask how it comes about that this timid creature ever ventured to those inhospitable heights, even though she were charged with the finding of Don José. To ask this is simply to ask the leading question, which can be answered only by saying, " this is opera." More fruitful is it to remark that Micaela need not be an insufferable bore. It has been affirmed that her appearances hold up the action, and that her creation was due to the advisability of introducing a light soprano into the score. This notwithstanding, the resourceful singer can make her something more than a puppet. The very intensity of Carmen's nature should help her to accomplish this. The chief danger lies in a too obvious exaggeration of Micaela's goodness, which can easily descend from that condition to the lesser and distressing one of goody-goodyness. But Micaela's music is of value. Her romance has been singled out by one writer as " the most effective and beautiful number in the work," and the character can be turned into one both interesting and pleasing, if it be delivered into the right hands.

Not much requires to be said of the rest of the cast. Frasquita and Mercedes may exist, as has been remarked, merely in order to participate in the ensembles. They are certainly thumbnail sketches, and as such incapable of extensive working-up in the matter of " business." Yet, like most thumbnail sketches, they will be good, middling or bad, according as the interpreters are good, middling or bad. While of the smuggling couple, Dancairo and Remendado, I speak with diffidence (never having met a smuggler in my life), I do not hesitate to say that they should *not* be transformed into funny men of the English music-hall pattern.

Leaving the story and the characters and coming to the music, one faces the question of the " Spanishness," real or pseudo, of the same. I have read that Spanish singers have not, on the whole, won such success in the part of Carmen as might have been expected. If this be strictly true, the circumstance may possess its own significance ; the Spanish singer may all the time be keenly conscious of the fact that the music never took root in the soil of Spain ; she may find it merely an elegant importation from France. As the attitude of the Spaniard is always likely to command a considerable amount of attention, I set down the words in which it has been described to me : the enlightened Spanish musician refuses to consider the music as genuinely Spanish, as representing the folk-music of the people. To call it a counterfeit may be to exaggerate, but it does not spring directly from the real heart of the popular songs.

Tiersot describes the method followed by Bizet, who, he writes, had recourse to the employment of popular Spanish melodies. He is careful to add, however, that Bizet did not limit himself to the borrowing of folk-themes. What the composer did was to assimilate the forms, the rhythms, and accents of the songs, after which he created new themes, wherein the Spanish melody came to life again, wherein his own personality is evident. " The only exception," continues Tiersot, " is the habanera," though he says of the last entra'cte what many must have thought—so strongly imprinted is it with the character of the Spanish dance, one almost hesitates to believe that Bizet composed it. Tiersot confesses never to have found it in any collection ; Gaudier, on the contrary, asserts that Bizet has here made use of a *polo*, sung by a serenading student in a musical piece called *El Criado Fingido*, composed in 1804 by Manuel Garcia, the father of Malibran and Mme. Viardot.[1]

In spite of all that can be said on this as on other topics, the picturesqueness and flavour which runs through the score may pretty safely be attributed to Bizet's inspiration. One has only to mention the seguidilla and the *chanson bohème* to show how finely Bizet got the very accent, the very tone and colour, for which the scenes yearn ; and I agree wholeheartedly with Tiersot when he praises the modulations of the seguidilla, which, he remarks, follow the stage movements ingeniously. But perhaps too much has already been made of this aspect of the opera. To the Spanish specialist it may not be Spanish at all ; he may see in it a mythical Spain, so coloured by French spectacles that it proclaims an origin east of the Pyrenees ; he may see in it a proof that, despite the celebrated *mot* of a French king, the range of mountains does still exist. To some it may be Spanish with several and important reservations. To others, again, the matter is no doubt one of supreme unimportance. I myself do not believe that it is a Spanish score, if the adjective be used in a rigorously scientific sense ; and I do not for one moment believe that Bizet's in-

---

[1] See Paul Landormy's interesting comments on this point in his *Bizet*, and 20 *Chants Populaires Espagnols*, arranged by Joaquin Nin, Vol. II. p. 39.

tention was to provide a Spanish score in this sense.
We come back finally to the composer, as we
ought. How much the work owes to Spain, and
the nature of that probable, possible, or doubtful
indebtedness are legitimate subjects of inquiry,
which possess their interest and will likely chain
the curious to prolonged speculation. Let them
not be led away from the fact that *Carmen* is, first
and last, the creation of Bizet. The Spain to
which it introduces us may never have existed.
It is a living Spain, for all that, seen through a
temperament. It paints in glowing colours that
sun-kissed land, and by its warmth and fervour, its
dramatic power and picturesqueness breathes life
into the Spain we behold. By doing so, it causes
us to ask if the method of the artist, with his
imagination, may not achieve something denied
to extremely precise and literal folk. Mr Pick-
wick is far more real than the man who lives next
door.[1]

Gaudier remarks that the merit exhibited by
Bizet is not to be found in plan or method, but
in the quality of the musical utterance, in the
suitability of the musical phrase to the poetical
phrase, to the situation and to the sentiment.
Few people are likely to quarrel with him.
Structurally, *Carmen* differs very little from the
traditional *opéra-comique*. In this respect it is
far from a revolutionary work. There are airs,

[1] For the views of Joaquin Turina, see *Le Courier Musical*,
1st March, 1925.

duets, ensembles and choruses whose bounds are definitely set ; they can be detached from the context. Once or twice, as in the *moderatos* which break in upon the seguidilla, Bizet seems to be pointing the way to a greater freedom. Those who speak of his having carried the *opèra-comique* to the portals of grand opera may have such moments in mind. Putting them aside, one sees in *Carmen* an opera laid out as many others of its kind have been laid out.

We have to look elsewhere for novelty, com-pelling attraction, and other virtues worthy of remark. They lie, of course, in the music itself.[1] How well it accords with the story, the characters and the atmosphere, will best be realised if I say that Bizet has written *Carmen* once and for all. He who penned another work on this subject would incur a grave risk ; another *Carmen* is, frankly, unthinkable. The opera, to be sure, is innocent of the music that ministers to grey moods, or appeases the troubled soul. Such is called for neither by the theme, nor by the turns it takes. And some parts are stronger than others. We all have our preferences in this matter, as that first audience of 1875 had its preferences. But I imagine that one would be hard put to it if asked to place a finger upon any spot where the music takes a tragic dip and descends to the nether

---

[1] The high value of some of the *Carmen* themes must have been brought home to those who were fortunate enough to hear Busoni play his imaginative and poetical *Chamber Phantasy* on the opera.

regions of the vastly inferior. *Carmen* is unique in two senses. It is unique in the realm of opera ; there is no work quite like it. It is unique also in that it stands head and shoulders above anything else Bizet produced. This singularity causes me to refrain from throwing in my lot with those who weep over the might-have-beens, as it causes me to seek a reason for the manifest superiority. Admitting the mysterious aspect of artistic creation, which always baffles the analyst, I think that the success of *Carmen* arises in large measure from the meeting of the man and the work. The man was by nature cut out for the work. With such a nature he was well able to extract the last drop of emotion from it. This preliminary advantage is apt to be either overlooked or minimised. It is a real advantage, nevertheless. Sympathy will take you further than considerateness, however painstaking. It took Bizet, who threw himself heart and soul into the Spanish story of the gypsy, very far.

I have said enough to let the reader know that I place *Carmen* high by reason of the quality of its inspiration, the attraction of its themes, the handling of its ideas, and the musicianship displayed throughout. There is characterisation, too, skilfully devised, as can be seen by comparing the music of Carmen with that of Micaela, the music of Don José with that of Escamillo, the smugglers' chorus with the choruses which open the last act. If any doubt linger in the reader's mind about the quality of the Escamillo music, a few moment's thought as to its fitness should lay that doubt to rest. We remember the story about Bizet's discarding an earlier version of the toreador's song in order to substitute the one we know so well, and that Lamoureux told how, after having finished the popular number, Bizet said, " Well, they asked for rubbish, and they've got it." At the same time, I feel that more needs to be said ; that, taking into the reckoning the character of Escamillo, his calling, and the circumstances of his arrival at the inn, the music is not at all " out of key." I own at once that the song is not distinguished, only to ask who in the wide world wants here the kind of music that commonly earns that epithet. As Tiersot declares, the swagger of a toreador does not accommodate itself so badly to a bright and rhythmic refrain, even if it does lack distinction. " I am not sure," adds the French critic, " whether our art is not in peril through being too ' *distingué*.' "

The very first bars, which plunge us into the bustle and excitement of Seville *en fête*, are thoroughly reassuring. Take this music to pieces ; it yields little to the analytical eye ; no extraordinary theme, no extraordinary harmony, nothing at all extraordinary in the technical sense. Still, it has in it not only animation, which can easily be infused into a score, but what strikes us as the *right kind* of animation. Those processional strains, with their well-marked theme and swing, hit off the scene with such success that we recognise in them the authentic musical expression of the same. I am genuinely sorry for those who do not get a thrill when the orchestra attacks the first bar of the opera.

As though to emphasise the dual aspect of the story, its splendour and its squalor, the motto theme of the work—Nietzsche's "epigram on passion "—comes at the end of the prelude. While one cannot speak of subtlety, the juxtaposition of the martial and the menacing is sufficiently impressive. A jaunty opening chorus is soon interrupted by some tripping measures when Micaela appears, and after a resumption of it we arrive at the lively boys' chorus, which, with its sprightly little subject, is Bizet through and through. Equally typical I find the earlier part of the cigarette makers' chorus—even the modulation that disconcerted some hearers in 1875 ; to this succeeds a graceful melody, displaced by a staccato passage at " *le doux parler.*" The entrance of Carmen occurs to a version of the motto theme just mentioned, a theme likely to be recognised and remembered on account of what has been aptly called " its sinister beauty." This sinister beauty arises from the employment of the augmented second, an interval often found in gypsy music. The habanera, one of the purple patches, follows. The motto theme returns as Carmen throws the cassia flower at José, and a superb phrase of passionate intensity, given out by the orchestra, terminates the scene.

The duet for José and Micaela is of a melting character, and seldom fails to elicit the approval of the audience. It is not by any means the highest point in the opera, though one may concede that Bizet supplied music quite in keeping with the situation and the sentiment. A tumultuous chorus, wherein the workers make excited comments upon the quarrel which has taken place in the factory, is more happily inspired. It has been said, and with complete truth, that, for all its stir and turmoil, the piece never ceases to be musical. Carmen's impudent " tra-la-la " is imbued with the right spirit, as is the seguidilla, which ought to be sung with more softness and lightness than singers always bring to it. This number is from first to last a thing of beauty and delight. The flute gives out the piquant theme ; this is soon taken up by the voice, the orchestra supplying a light staccato accompaniment suggestive of guitar thrummings. As the song proceeds, the flute makes its voice heard again when, an octave higher, it delicately imitates the notes which Carmen has just sung to the words, " *Oui mais toute seule en s'ennuie* " ; and flute and voice cross one another at the delicious " *Qui veut mon âme.*" The finale is of modest dimensions. It opens with a *fugato* based on the theme of the quarrel (violoncelli, violas, second violins, then first violins). This leads to a reintroduction of

239

the habanera refrain which, dying away, yields to an *allegro vivace* based on the music of the dispute.

The prelude to Act II shows what Bizet could do in a few bars. Every note of the clever and simple piece bears the stamp of his personality ; it might, indeed, almost be called a microcosm of Bizet's art at its best. The theme that furnishes the text is the kind of theme to which Bizet so often invites attention ; a short, staccato one asking for the lightness of treatment and scoring that are so cunningly given to it. The bassoons announce the subject, which is the air of the dragoons of Alcala. After some characteristic play with a little four-bar phrase—very Bizet-like this —the subject returns in the clarinet, accompanied by a falling counterpoint in the bassoon. Bizet concludes the tiny prelude by allotting fragments of the air to the wood-winds, while the notes of the dominant and tonic *ppp* bring the piece to a close. These few bars, and there are only ninety of them, should be placed beside the music of *L'Arlésienne* inasmuch as they have character, inasmuch as they reveal the personality of the composer, and inasmuch as they prove his ability to express himself in small compass.

The *chanson bohème*, which opens the act, has plenty of colour, spirit, and " go " ; an alluring number, which owes its success to the persistent rhythm, the sudden and arresting modulations, the *pianissimo* refrain and the orchestral dressing.

Escamillo arrives to a chorus that is *not*, and should *not* be, *distingué*. It merely prepares the ground for the toreador's song ; of this I have said something above. Gaudier mentions the carelessness of some baritones who do not trouble to distinguish between the D flat, which occurs in the first part of the melody (at the words, " *car avec le soldat* "), and the D natural which occurs on the repetition (at the words, " *du haut en bas* ") ; a word of warning not by any means without its justification. At the end, we happen upon a concession to popular taste in the form of a curious addition. Mercedes, Frasquita and Carmen looking at Escamillo, one after the other, utter " *l'amour.*" Escamillo answers by uttering the same words, doubtless giving to each utterance its own emphasis, though reserving the note of conviction for the last. Whether this interpolation really augments the effectiveness of the scene is more than a little doubtful ; it is frequently cut out.

We are now at the quintet for the three women, Frasquita, Mercedes, and Carmen, and the two smugglers, Dancairo and Remendado, an excellent thing in its way, with a pertness, ingenuity and gaiety, altogether becoming. This vocal scherzo is effortless music, which might have run off the very point of Bizet's pen. He has well distributed the interest among the voices and given to the orchestral part a life of its own. The song of José in the wings does not call for special mention, except to say that in performance it does not always end in tune. Carmen dances before him, accompanying herself with the castanets. The subject, I suspect, was framed in order to accommodate itself to the bugle-call, which gradually forces itself into prominence. The heated outbursts of Carmen and the sad pleadings of José, couched spiritually in different keys, are excellently depicted. We should be made to feel the difference between them more acutely than we generally do in the theatre. Here, for a brief space, we come face to face with Bizet the dramatist in his stride, and this moving scene is worked up in masterly manner to the introduction of the flower song, where the motto theme under a threatening *tremolo* tells us how all this ghastly business is going to end. While the flower song holds up the action for a few moments, it would be wrong to regard it only as a tempting tit-bit for the egotistical tenor, because it is in reality an integral part of the drama. To dismiss it simply as a pretty piece of writing is to tell but half the story. The opening has great lyrical beauty ; many composers would do well if they wrote a phrase as exquisite in contour. Observe, however, that behind the grace and fervour there lurks a latent passion. The full value of the song is not only in its grace or in its waxing devotion, conspicuous as they are ; consider how the music lays bare José's sentiments ; consider its appositeness to the critical moment. Of the ending,

242

"*Carmen, je t'aime,*" something has been chronicled in these pages. It does not worry us nowadays, though it seems to worry some tenors, who do not keep the pitch.

Only a word or two need be devoted to the remainder of this act. Carmen's invitation to José to flee with her to the mountains is made to some light and attractive music in 6/8 time. This is broken into by a very fine dramatic passage that begins with José's contemptuous refusal to desert. The complexion of the whole changes with the beginning of the finale, and it is instructive to note how Bizet, in a page or two, passes from an intense situation, culminating in a *tutta forza*, to the badinage of *Carmen's* "*Bel officier.*" The chorus to Liberty is simply a conventional finish, based on the theme we heard when Carmen tempted her companion to the mountains.

I have already said all that is necessary regarding the prelude to Act III ; it was originally destined for *L'Arlésienne.* I do not think one need reproach Bizet for any lack of conscience in putting this number into the *Carmen* score. All that he wanted was a few measures of a reposeful nature, and this little intermezzo fulfils his demands. The smugglers' scene opens with a march played on the flute, the lower strings providing a staccato accompaniment. From the very first bar, Bizet has been successful in giving his music the right atmosphere. The theme is a small light-stepping one, oft repeated, and it leads directly into a chorus which, from the technical point of view, is the most difficult in the opera, and from the historical point of view the most original. I imagine that few choruses to be found in earlier *opéras-comiques* show as much harmonic freedom. The trio of the cards follows. After a few introductory ejaculations, Frasquita and Mercedes together sing a gracious melody that pipes the good fortune awaiting them. They prattle along merrily until Carmen proceeds to read her fate. A variant of the motto theme is played *pianissimo*. Carmen turns up diamonds, then spades. The motto theme returns ; Carmen knows that she is doomed to die. A dark-coloured page of weighty and monotonous chords puts all hope to flight, and points as with a finger to the tragic end which Destiny has in store. A bright ensemble is now thrown in in order to allow the smugglers to depart. It has been stated that this number was meant for *L'Arlésienne*. Its purpose is clear enough. To put it bluntly, Bizet had to make room for Micaela. He did this by interpolating the ensemble in question, which is in his liveliest manner. The counterpoint sung by Carmen against the melody allotted to Frasquita and Mercedes is very effective, if executed with the neatness the composer obviously had in mind, and the two bars ushering in the return of the subject must have been a surprise to an audience in 1875.

Micaela's air has been enthusiastically praised,

and dismissed with some heat for its banality. Dramatically, all that need be claimed for it is that, by reason of its suavity, tranquillity, and prevailing atmosphere, it impresses the character of the village maiden upon the hearer anew. Structurally, it maintains its contact with tradition. In character, it has nothing in common with the rest of the work. It is a conventional production, but a conventional production in no bad sense. The romantic opening on the horn is of an extreme picturesqueness, and happily indicates the yearning which fills Micaela's breast.

Let us pass on. Duels are not commonly the best parts of operas. The one which occurs between José and Escamillo is no better, or worse, than most. Micaela pleads with José to return to his dying mother in strains that have been made known in the first act, and Carmen immediately hurls her sarcasms at the unfortunate creature. The contrast between the two women is cunningly manipulated. With the outbursts of José—among the finest things in the opera—the scene hastens to its close. The orchestra plays a fragment of the motto theme twice. From the distance comes Escamillo's voice singing the refrain of his song. A few subdued measures based on the smugglers' chorus ring down the curtain.

The most Spanish of the intermezzi opens the last act, which, apart from the fête music at the start, is almost entirely a duet. Observe the two divisions into which this act naturally falls ; the first all joy and light-heartedness, the second all tragedy. In order to heighten the effect and emphasise the contrast, both parts must be carefully treated. After the imposing spectacle, Escamillo addresses Carmen tenderly, and she responds in phrases equally tender. A charmingly irresponsible theme heralds the arrival of Frasquita and Mercedes, when they come to warn Carmen against José. This over, the ground is clear for the culminating point of the opera, the finest piece of writing Bizet accomplished— pointed, sincere, and moving. The scene is not of great length, but it rapidly gains in intensity as it proceeds. José's pleading (" *Carmen, il est temps encore* ") soon turns into a cry more passionate (" *Mais moi, Carmen, je t'aime encore* "), which ends with an unbridled outburst. Carmen's insolent and courageous answers are of immense power. As the music gathers strength Bizet almost mercilessly throws up the darkness of the tragedy by introducing the spirited and joyful theme of the procession, now sung by the spectators at the bullfight. In order to show how this reacts on José, the first of these acclamations is followed by a *pianissimo* allegro ; the suppressed chromatic bass hints at the madness thus kindled in the man's heart. The second of them prepares the way for a broad *fortissimo* announcement of the motto theme, several times repeated. Carmen's

BIZET

final refusal to have anything to do with José
and José's last desperate act are followed by the
refrain of Escamillo's song—Fate's gesture of
derision. As might be expected, the motto theme
claims the orchestra in the end, and by doing so
imparts a feeling of finality. Thus terminates a
masterpiece, written by the man born to write
it ; an opera which came from the heart and goes
to the heart ; an opera in which there is not a dull
bar ; an opera free from the slightest taint of
doctrine or didacticism ; an opera well described by
Puccini, when, twenty years ago, he summed it up
as " the most complete and most vibrant that has
been produced in recent years." Had he composed nothing else, Bizet would be as assured of
fame as he would be deserving of it. In the
happily-chosen words of an English critic,
" *Carmen* is one of the treasures of music."

For the sake of completeness, *Vasco da Gama*
and *Noë* should here be noticed. *Vasco da Gama*
is an unequal, ambitious, and immature production
and as such of purely historical interest. Like
L'Arlésienne, it contains a bolero, but it does
not show that any critical power the composer
possessed at the time of its composition was
very seriously exercised. As already stated, *Noë*
has not been performed in France. The ballet
plays a great part in the last act and introduces
extracts from *Djamileh*, together with *Le Coccinelle*,
a song written to words by Victor Hugo.

Apart from *Carmen*, *L'Arlésienne* is generally

247

and justly accounted the finest work of Bizet.
That a selection of the music should so frequently
be found in concert programmes may be construed as a tribute to its picturesqueness and
melodiousness, for not every visitor to the concert
hall is conversant with Daudet's piece. This is
concerned with a young farmer, Frédéri, who
is violently enamoured of a charming woman
belonging to Arles. He is about to wed her when
he discovers that she is not worthy of his affection.
In his despair he pays court to Vivette, an attractive girl whom he has known from his boyhood.
Vivette loves him passionately, but Frédéri cannot
forget the fascinating Arlésienne, who becomes an
obsession. His constant thought of her unhinges
his mind, and on the night of St. Eloi, when the
countryside is making merry and the peasants
are dancing the gay farandole, he jumps out of a
window, falls into the courtyard of the farm, and
is killed.

Bizet's participation took the form of a series
of tiny numbers of varying, but always modest,
dimensions. In the writing of them he did not
shut his eyes to the part his music had to play ;
he was very careful not to exceed the bounds
dictated by the occasion. I can think of no other
score of a similar nature, at least from French
hands, which is so successful. A hearing of
L'Arlésienne convinces us that what the composer set out to do he did without strain. The
action passes in Provence, and Bizet very naturally

has drawn upon the songs and dances of that delightful land. Thus the overture is based upon the tough and rousing theme of *La Marche dei Rei*, a Provençal air. For two reasons the choice was wise. The theme itself is a good, rhythmic one of strong accents and bursting vitality ; it is moreover, a workable theme likely to suggest interesting treatment to the musical mind. In the second act appears a folksong, *Er doù Guet*, and the familiar farandole is merely a version of the *Danso dei Chivau-Frus*. It should also be observed that the chorus in F Sharp minor partakes of the character of a bolero. As those who have heard the music in concert know, there is much charm, piquancy, and atmosphere in it. The overture, with its delightful variations upon the aforementioned *Marche dei Rei*, which dominates the whole, the minuet (there can be no doubt as to its composer's name), the carillon, the farandole, the tiny adagietto for strings—these are the most important, as they are the most popular sections ; but the short andantino in B Major which forms the twentieth number should be mentioned, if only because of the very Schumannesque contour of its melody. It is remarkable that both here and in Grieg's incidental music to Ibsen's *Peer Gynt* we find a very brief fragment scored for strings only, and that in each case the composer has demonstrated his ability to achieve much, not only with the simplest of means, but within a very limited compass.

Nothing save a worship of sheer bulk will stand in the way of a proper appreciation of the *Death of Ase* and the adagietto of *L'Arlésienne*. In these pages there is not a bar on which to " crag the mind," not a bar to set the controversial pen racing over white paper. Let us not be deceived. Where many others have failed Grieg and Bizet have succeeded. In his adagietto Bizet captured a rare beauty. I know many works ponderous in their science, of ambitious scope and disastrous length, that contain less true music. ˙I repeat, Bizet was often at his best in little things ; as witness this adagietto and the *Carmen* entr'actes. So artfully did he frame them, so easy was he when operating within self-imposed bounds, that he must have felt as Wordsworth felt about the sonnet :

> " and hence for me,
> In sundry moods, 'twas pastime to be bound
> Within the sonnet's scanty plot of ground."

As *L'Arlésienne* is scored for a small orchestra of a somewhat unusual kind, the various instruments which comprise it should be enumerated— seven violins, one viola, five violoncelli, two double-basses, two flutes, one oboe (taking the cor anglais), one clarinet, two bassoons, one saxophone, two horns, kettledrum, and piano. I have alluded to the three suites. In the one arranged by him, which is the third, Sir Landon Ronald takes his material from the first and second, but so sets

it out as to throw into vivid relief the most
important ideas contained in the work.

The spirit of the man who wrote *Roma* was very
willing, but I question if he had really the symphonic temperament. That he never tried his
hand at a sonata has been duly observed, and,
maybe, the omission is at bottom a weighty confession. I believe that Bizet really loved *Roma*
and that he took pains to make it a creditable
contribution to the music of the concert hall. If
it is not all that he hoped for, we must take refuge
in the truth that he was primarily a dramatic
composer, and that, being so, he could not accommodate himself to the needs of the occasion with
all the ease and completeness which are the first
essentials for success. The most interesting
portions of the work are the scherzo and the
carnival. The scherzo is founded on a vivacious
theme to which the composer adheres faithfully
throughout. Towards the end there are one or
two clever and unexpected modulations that might
have come from Schubert. The trio forms a
contrast, as it is of a reposeful nature with a good
singing subject. It terminates very happily in a
manner that, curiously enough, again brings the
name of Schubert to mind. The carnival, an
allegro vivacissimo, starts with a fussy little theme,
accompanied by staccato chords ; it is soon displaced by a very Italian melody in thirds. These
two subjects have more than a little of the true
carnival spirit about them and seem to belong to

the merrymaking South. The second subject
proper, *ben sostenuto et cantabile*, is of a more
vigorous type, and not particularly Southern in
its complexion. Its choice was probably dictated
by the composer's desire to obtain the requisite
variety. The three ideas jostle one another in a
restless sort of fashion, and the suite finishes with
an *fff* announcement of the broad and singing
theme given out by the entire orchestra. The
opening *allegro* and the solo movement seem to me
to be somewhat lacking in distinction.

Patrie owes its origin to Pasdeloup, who asked
Bizet, Massenet and Guiraud, each to write
specially for him an overture he would perform
during the season of 1873–1874 ; an invitation
to which Bizet responded with the work just mentioned, Massenet with *Phèdre*, and Guiraud with
a concert overture. *Patrie* is not orthodox in the
matter of form. It is best designated as a descriptive and dramatic overture. The structure
is determined by the series of pictures the composer desired to introduce. No doubt, memories
of the war were present in his thoughts when he
wrote it. The overture is in C minor and major,
and scored for full orchestra. With that of the
Rakoczy march the opening theme has an obvious
kinship. There is a certain chivalrous quality
about this opening, and one can almost see, in the
mind's eye, troops of dark-skinned warriors riding
over the Hungarian plains. This is succeeded
by a bold subject, through which runs a vein of

patriotic sentiment. For a moment, we are arrested by a call to arms. The patriotic note, sounded again, but with great force and conviction, leads to an andante in A minor, wherein the violoncelli play an elegaic melody full of feeling. The sorrowful accents bring, in their turn, a graceful and flowing theme in the major, given to the clarinets, oboes and violas. After being treated for some little time, the sweet reposefulness is broken into by a curious section, where the original theme appears above a moving chromatic bass, as if to indicate that trouble is abroad. Once more comes a call to arms, vigorously announced by the brass. The patriotic subject now reappears in all its glory and brings the overture to a close with an eloquent promise of victory.

Bizet's piano music is not very widely known, and does not therefore contribute much to his fame. Of his efforts in this field the series of pictures which go by the name of *Jeux d'Enfants* is by far the most attractive. The writing of such unpretentious melodies must have been a labour of love, if one dare judge by the results of that labour, for Bizet satisfied the demands made upon him. We see here a delicious collection of miniatures written with a finely pointed pen. The composer says what he ought to say ; he says it with a simplicity and directness suitable to the subjects ; he does not, and for this let us be truly thankful, say too much. But we ought, in addition, to acknowledge that he did not confuse the childlike with the childish. The pieces are an invitation to the child's wonderful world, not music for children. The invitation is properly pressing and tempting, and the play of the little ones so cleverly depicted that he who cannot enter into the spirit of it must, indeed, be a churlish fellow. Technically, there is nothing to say about such a piece as *La Poupée* ; melodically and harmonically, it is all very plain sailing. But this confession made, we are thrown back on the plain fact that the music of the naïve berceuse *does* meet the case, *does* capture the right mood in that it is drawn to a small scale and has no deep roots, precisely because it happens to be concerned with a doll. This graceful effusion and its companions should be read as further evidence of Bizet's gifts in the rôle of miniaturist. Take, for example, the march called *Trompette et Tambour* ; this, like the final galop, *Le Bal*, strikes me as very typical of one side, and that not the least attractive, of Bizet's talent. To do it justice, we must confess that the march is something more than so many rhythmic measures which serve their turn. It is emphatically a march of mock soldiers, whose weapons will be put away in a play-box before the clock strikes eight ; it sounds the note of a nursery heroism, easily dissipated by the wind whistling in the chimney or some story about a grizzly bear. The tripping melody, *Les Quatre Coins*, and the expressive one of that delicious Lilliputian duo *Petite Marie, Petite Femme*,

are in the same case. They are not just so much
music written under pretty titles ; they are carefully worked cameos that belong by right to the
authentic nursery world. In similar manner, I
might speak of every number, only to say, in the
end, that I find the entire set happily conceived
and executed. Never does Bizet, like a clumsy
adult, step without the frontiers of the child's
domain. Even where the subject sanctions the
expression of a pretty sentiment, as in the noc-
turne, *Colin-Maillard*, he is not caught unawares.
More I need hardly say. The work makes no
pretence to be other than a string of trifles, but
they are musical trifles that have a genuine claim
on our regard. Mesdemoiselles Marguerite de
Bauelieu and Fanny Gouin should have felt
pleased when they learned that *Jeux d'Enfants*
bore their names upon the title page. The circumstances in which the *Petite Suite d'Orchestre*,
consisting of five numbers of *Jeux d'Enfants*, was
produced have been described. It remains only
to mention that the suite in question was performed
for the first time in London at a Philharmonic
Concert on the 3rd of May, 1888, under the
directorship of Sir (then Mr.) Frederic H. Cowen.

It is to be questioned if the other piano works
of Bizet reveal him at anything like his best,
certainly a curious phenomenon when we remember his expert talent. To take a case in
point, the *Chasse Fantastique*, which is dedicated
to Marmontel, cannot by any reckoning be put

high. It belongs to the swollen category of superficial descriptive pieces, is brilliant and flashy in a way that used to commend itself to parlour virtuosi bent on astonishing the family circle, but at no point does it rise above the commonplace ; it is like a " Tam o' Shanter " without Tam, Cutty Sark, or the poet's genius. The *Variations Chromatiques* are inscribed to Stephen Heller. With them Bizet owned to being pleased and, in a letter to Galabert of July, 1868, he spoke of the " audacious treatment " he had given the theme. The variations are neither extensive nor uncommonly arresting, there being but seven and a not very satisfactory coda. The Bizet we know leaps out of the page only once, at the fourth variation, whose daintiness it would be ungracious not to acknowledge. No more inspiring, *Les Chants du Rhin* are a set of six pieces on verses by Méry. *Ce beau fleuve* as a source of inspiration to a Frenchman impresses us as more than a trifle curious. I assume that at the period of composition Bizet was visited by an attack of that species of romanticism which looked upon the Rhine, not as a bearer of burdens or as a political problem, but as a home of sentiment, or a dark and mysterious being who harboured sprites and fairies and threw a spell over the dreamy wanderer. For the most part, these Rhine songs resemble a feeble echo of Mendelssohn. The best of them is No. 3, *Les Rêves*, which is based on a graceful and singing theme ; No. 6, *Le Retour*,

dedicated to Saint-Saëns, is only poor salon music.
I am unable to place these pieces on the same level
as that attained by Mendelssohn's *Songs without
words,* though Marmontel is able to do so. On
the other hand, I agree with most authorities that
Bizet's best song is *Les Adieux de l'hôtesse Arabe,*
and wonder why, in view of its effectiveness, it is
so strangely neglected by singers ; only once have
I heard it sung in public. *Le Gascon,* a lively
song to words by Catulle Mendès, also merits
attention as being typical. The fourth bar of the
introduction recalls the identical bar of chorus,
Quant au douanier.

For more than one reason I have hitherto said
nothing of what may for convenience be called
" The Wagner Question," in so far as it affects
Bizet's story. It seemed to me that this question
deserved a place to itself ; it seemed also that no
place more fitting could be found than at the end
of a survey of his musical achievement. Much
space has been devoted to the topic by all writers
upon Bizet's career and work. However startling this may appear at the first blush, it is not
startling when one knows that Bizet was called
Wagnerian, and that the adjective appears often
to have been on the tongues or at the point of the
pens of some judges. Bizet and Wagner—there
seems to us to be very little, if anything, in common
between the men. It is worth while to examine
the question in order to find out what those who
employed the adjective really meant by it. Gala-

bert tells us that Bizet revealed to him the beauties
of *Tannhäuser* and *Lohengrin* at the piano.   These
two works, together with *The Flying Dutchman*,
were probably the only ones of Wagner available
in French at the time.   While there is not much
to be gathered from Galabert's laconic entry,
something of greater moment awaits the reader
of a letter written in April, 1869.   In the course
of this Bizet talks of *Rienzi*, which he had just
heard.   He calls it a badly-constructed work,
having only one rôle, that of the hero ;   he condemns the score as a " *mélange* " of Italian motifs,
finds it the music of decadence rather than the
music of the future, and pours contempt on the
style, which he describes as both bizarre and inferior.   From the foregoing it will be seen that
Bizet knew *Rienzi*, *Tannhäuser* and *Lohengrin*.
How much more did he know ?   I must ask this
question because the answer to it will necessarily
affect our estimate of those who spoke of the
"*farouche Wagnérien.*"   A letter to Mme. Halévy,
dated the 29th of May, 1871, contains references
to the eminent German.   The pity is that the
references are merely of a general nature.   Bizet
owns that the charm of Wagner's music is in-
describable ;   he sees the German spirit of the
Nineteenth Century incarnated in this man ;   he
regards Wagner as a person of such insolent demeanour that criticism cannot touch his heart,
" admitting that he has a heart, which I doubt."
Wagner's music, he confesses, is not the music of

the future, but the music of all time, because it is great ; if he thought that he were imitating Wagner he would not write another note. So far so good. We are still left wondering how much of Wagner Bizet knew. In the preface to the Lacombe letters Hugues Imbert asks what Bizet would have thought of *The Ring* and *Parsifal* had he been able to make the journey to Bayreuth. This serves to remind us that the Frenchman did not know the Wagner, or at least all the Wagner, we know. The first performance of *The Ring* took place in 1876, that of *Parsifal* in 1882. Bizet died in 1875. It is clear, therefore, that much of the fuller glory which contributes to Wagner's fame did not burst upon the world till after Bizet's death. Tiersot, for his part, puts the case in a nutshell. It was enough for Bizet to declare in peremptory tones that Wagner had genius ; the declaration rendered him suspect.

It should be understood that the adjective Wagnerian is of a fluctuating significance. In its turn, it has been both a flattering and a damning one. Its significance is relative to the knowledge and bias of the person who uses it. Before we gain any light we must know who uses it, and why he does so. Pigot says that on his return from Rome the accusation of Wagnerism was first thrown at Bizet—a strange admission—and it evidently burst out again with some vehemence after *Djamileh*. How did Bizet so early come under this spell ? How far were those who at

any time reproached him acquainted with Wagner?
To call a man a Wagnerian may, as I have suggested, mean one of many things, among them a
slavish follower and an enlightened individual,
who takes legitimate advantage of new things
accomplished, fresh fields thrown open to posterity. The gainsayers, we may be quite sure,
meant nothing very complimentary or creditable,
and that, perhaps, is all that one can say about
them. They did not like Bizet's music, or, for
reasons of their own, proclaimed that they did
not like it (which is not quite the same thing);
and, looking round for a catch-phrase, fixed upon
that blessed word we are now considering. One
cannot for a moment believe that the people who
chattered in this way had the smallest idea of
those things for which Wagner stood. Wagner
was a kind of bogey man who lived beyond the
frontier, a vast monstrosity who stood for chaos
and cacophony. The quickest and surest way
to pooh-pooh a composer was to establish his
spiritual kinship with this terrifying ogre. It was
not enough to such people that things are not what
they seem ; the edict gaily went forth that they
are not what they are.

All this tedious and trivial foolishness is shown
up by Bizet's music itself. The music of Bizet
does not resemble the music of Wagner. A
comparison of the one with the other yields the
most conclusive proof that the gainsayers were
talking loosely and incorrectly, so loosely and

incorrectly that they deserve no courtesy from us. If they were ignorant, they were grievously at fault in using the word Wagnerian at all ; if they had dipped into Wagner's available scores, they had only done so to misunderstand them ; if, by chance, they did understand them, they were as full of prejudice as an egg is of meat. One can say as much after attempting to recreate the historical circumstances in which this strange little controversy was fought out. Bizet may have been a good, a bad, or an indifferent composer ; he was not a Wagnerian one. I do not think he was a Wagnerian, even in the limited, later Nineteenth Century French sense. Eliminate *The Ring* and *Parsifal*, which he did not hear, he yet does not approach Wagner.

The last lines of this story have a sublime irony. At the man's coat-tails there were superficial dillettanti, who found satisfaction in telling one another, parrot-like, that Bizet wrote Wagnerian music ; in other words, outrageous music. It was of the same man that Nietzsche wrote so eulogistically in his essay, " The Case of Wagner." He praises Bizet because he finds in him a refuge from, and an antithesis to, Wagnerism ; he finds him the only man capable of turning humanity away from the dangerous road of Bayreuth ; he finds in the composer of *Carmen* the man able to mediterraneanise music. With Bizet's work, he says, one departs from the humid north and all the mists of the Wagnerian world ; it has the

dry air and *limpidezza* of warm climes. The gods
must have smiled when they saw the *farouche
Wagnérian* hailed by a philosopher as a man who
stood far away from the dark and stormy haunts
of the Teuton genius, and praised enthusiastically
because he had wedded music in the sunny south.
One should not be deceived by Nietzsche's declarations on this point. Their chief value lies
in the fact that they let us see the workings of his
mind at the period of writing. They should be
read in the light of his previous musical odyssey.
That he did enjoy *Carmen* is beyond doubt, but
the psychologist would be able to explain the
extreme, eulogistic note which derives much of
its ardour and excessiveness not from an enjoyment of Bizet's music, but from a dislike of
Wagner's. Have we here, perchance, something
resembling Victor Hugo's exaltation of Beethoven,
which meant, as Romain Rolland has it, that the
great man of Germany was not Goethe ?

It is high time to disentangle Bizet from the
Bizet myth. I have attempted this in so far as
the *Carmen* production and its effect upon the
composer are concerned. There remains to say
only a few words of wider application ; a few
words touching upon Bizet's life and work viewed
as a whole.

In spite of the high-sounding, imperial names
he bore, he had in his composition none of the
rude stuff of which heroes and martyrs are
fashioned ; no grave Carlyle dwelt behind that

genial exterior. He was not a pioneer. He never took up his spade in order to break new ground ; he was not haunted by the persistent and commanding curiosity which impels men to set out upon hazardous expeditions and embark upon difficult adventures. We might almost go the length of saying that beneath all the inconsistencies and waverings, to which I have called attention, there was an unbroken consistency, the unbroken consistency of an unstable catholicity. The boy was unusually amenable to discipline. Apt as a child, he submitted willingly to the parental rule. At the Conservatoire, that is during the feverish period of fermentation, he found his masters acceptable, his work interesting, his studies engrossing. Not, perhaps, the typical good boy of the class, he was neither rebellious nor, by reason of contrariness of spirit, a thorn in the magisterial flesh. If it be the business of academies to be academic and of conservatoires to conserve, this natural submission tells us much. He returned from Rome to write music that was not by any means a dangerous challenge to the proprieties. We mark the tokens of his indebtedness, now to Rossini (*Don Procopio*), now to Gounod (*Les Pêcheurs de Perles*), now to Mendelssohn and Schumann (the piano pieces), and recall his complacency in the matter of the habanera and the toreador's song.

I cannot think of any innovation associated with his name, any startling technical discovery that can be accurately traced to daring speculation on his part. The passage which occurs in the smuggler's chorus of *Carmen*, at the words "*prends garde de faire un faux pas*," was probably diabolically harsh to the opera-going public of 1875, but I hesitate to affirm that its like had never previously been heard. If he subjected the form of the *opéra-comique* to a greater strain than it had hitherto borne, that is, of course, something to be noticed ; and we are not likely to forget how Marmontel dwells upon the surprising ingenuity exhibited in the scoring of his last work. Nietzsche enjoyed this orchestration, which came from a man who regarded Berlioz's treatise as a *vade mecum*, and held it true that a piece can be scored only by its composer. Such facts do not obscure the issue. The eclecticism of Bizet is so evident that one cannot mistake it. He has been called a composer of the "*avant-garde*." He was so attached to tradition that, as Emile Vuillermoz writes, certain critics called him to order because of his concessions to the bad taste of the public.

Even *Carmen*, some will say, is indebted to Spain. I cannot accept this saying without making clear my conviction that, however much or little Bizet borrowed from this or that alien source, he did what Handel had done before him ; in the taking he made the thing his own. If possession be nine points of the law, such an assimilative faculty will fully exonerate the borrower. I concede the reminiscences and obligations of the earlier compositions. *Carmen* is personal—D'Indy was struck by its *new art;* and yet we vainly scrutinise it for the knotty points in which the larger aspect of Liszt is so prolific, we vainly put it under the microscope in order to fix upon problems that use up the midnight oil of the student and that adventurers are wont to throw in the face of their public. Stainer and Prout might have embraced the man without casting a slur upon their pedagogic respectability.

The truth is that Bizet was not deeply interested in the opening up of fresh paths. He worked with the tools and according to the methods handed down to him. Admitting this, let us hold the balance justly. Not all experimenters are interesting ; not all men in whom the crusading instinct is absent are dull. If Bizet offer nothing, or next to nothing, to the curiohunter, he does offer something to the vast body of musical folk. Leave his name out of the history of Nineteenth Century French music, you are at once conscious of a tragic blank. Galabert will not have it that he is the composer only of *L'Arlésienne* and *Carmen*, those two productions which, according to the pert Gauthier-Villars, are " *articles de Paris* " in the eyes of the foreigner. His admiration is broader-based than mine. But put the earlier works, if you are so minded, upon the shelf ; you are left with two masterpieces. Pharisee and snob, pedant and highbrow have here no proper material for their satire, no legitimate opening for their cheap jests. After half a century, *Carmen* not only holds its sway over the world of opera-goers ; its appeal is wider than ever. Brush away all the controversies, dismiss from your mind the petty factions, cease your hunt for the merely curious ; you have the score as it is, one of the brightest ornaments in the crown of French music. *Carmen* has had no successor, precisely because it is so personal, precisely because it owes its existence to Bizet himself. Somehow, we say, his life had been a tarrying and a preparation for this supremely fine thing. The word that comes to our lips as we think of it is the word with which Puccini and Sir Landon Ronald have described it—*Carmen* is complete.

There are heights that Bizet never reached, depths that he never plumbed. He had no residence above the snow-line of sublime thought. Through his pages we search fruitlessly for the deep, diapason note, the note that betokens the heroic sublimation of adversity. We can afford to acknowledge these truths, for we know full well that he left us something from which we would not willingly be parted ; we know that to reproach the rose for not being the oak is foolishness itself.

Debussy's art, says Romain Rolland in a suggestive passage, does not entirely represent French genius. There is another side to that genius of which the Pre-Raphaelite tells us nothing. This side Rolland fittingly designates as heroic action, the intoxication of reason and laughter, the passion for light—the France of Berlioz and Bizet. The composer of *L'Arlésienne* and *Carmen* is above all a poet of light and air, life and sunlight, who rescues us from the owlish haunts of barren science, and the sunless caves of dismal doctrine. French music has much to show which charms and delights ; it can claim little that is more charming and delightful than Bizet in his higher manifestations. The small fashionable toys of the hour leave us cold ; much that comes to us with high promises and large claims fails to move us. At such moments we shall seek joy and refreshment in the spontaneous melodies with which Bizet enriched his art.

APPENDIX A

List of Works

David, cantata. 1856
Clovis et Clothilde, cantata. 1857
Le Docteur Miracle, operetta in one act. 1857
Don Procopio, opéra-bouffe in two acts. 1859
Vasco de Gama, symphonic ode. 1860
Roma, suite. 1. Introduction and Allegro. 2. Scherzo. 3. Andante. 4. Carnival. 1861-1869
Les Pêcheurs de Perles, opera in three acts. 1863.
Les Chants du Rhin (six numbers). 1865
La Chasse Fantastique. 1865
Variations chromatiques de concert, for piano. 1868
La Jolie Fille de Perth, opera in four acts. 1867
Marlborough s'en va t'en guerre, operetta in four acts, of which the first only is by Bizet. 1867
Noë, biblical opera in three acts, left unfinished by Halévy and completed by Bizet. 1869
Djamileh, opéra-comique in one act. 1872
L'Arlésienne, incidental music to Alphonse Daudet's drama. 1872
Jeux d'Enfants, 12 pieces for piano duet—1872—of which five numbers were orchestrated by Bizet, and called " Petite Suite d'Orchestre." 1873
Patrie, dramatic overture. 1874
Carmen, opéra-comique in four acts. 1875
Piano Pieces—Songs—Transcriptions.

Works Destroyed or Not Completed

La Guzla de l'Emir, opera in one act. 1862
Ivan le Terrible, opera in five acts. 1865

APPENDIX A—*Continued*

La Coupe du Roi de Thulé, opera in five acts.   1868 ?
Calendal, opera in three acts.   1869 ?
Les Templiers, opera in five acts.   1869 ?
Clarissa Harlowe, opéra-comique in three acts.   1870
Grisélidis, opera in five acts.   1870
Le Cid, opera in five acts.   1873
Sainte Geneviève, oratorio.   1875

Critical Essay in *La Revue Nationale et Etrangère,* 3rd August 1867
    The foregoing list has been kindly revised by Madame Bizet-Straus, widow of the composer, expressly for this volume.

APPENDIX B

COMPARATIVE CHRONOLOGY

	GEORGES BIZET	OTHER FRENCH COMPOSERS	ITALIAN COMPOSERS	GERMAN COMPOSERS
1838	Born 25th Oct.	Berlioz's *Benvenuto Cellini*, 1838	Arrigo Boïto, born 1842	Wagner's *Rienzi*, 1842
1847	Enters Paris Conservatoire		Verdi's *Ernani*, 1844	Death of Mendelssohn, 1847
1857	*Le Docteur Miracle*, Prix de Rome	Gounod's *Sappho*, 1851	Verdi's *Rigoletto*, 1851 " *La Traviata*, 1853	Wagner's *Lohengrin*, 1850 Death of Schumann, 1856
1863	*Les Pêcheurs de Perles*	Gounod's *Faust*, 1859	Puccini born, 1858	Richard Strauss born 1864
1867	*La Jolie Fille de Perth.*	A. Thomas's *Mignon*, 1866	Verdi's *Don Carlos*, 1867	Wagner's *Tristan und Isolde*, 1865
1872	*Djamileh* *L'Arlésienne*	Death of Berlioz, 1869 Death of Auber, 1871	Verdi's *Aïda*, 1871 Boïto's *Mefistofele*, 1875	Wagner's *Die Meistersinger*, 1868 Foundation stone of Festspielhaus, Bayreuth, laid, 1872
1875	*Carmen* Died 3rd June			

APPENDIX C

BIBLIOGRAPHY

CAMILLE BELLAIGUE

Georges Bizet, sa vie et son œuvre. Delagrave, 1890

GEORGES BIZET

Lettres : Impressions de Rome (1857 – 1860). La Commune (1871). Preface by Louis Ganderax. Delagrave. 1909
Lettres à un ami (1865–1872). Introduction by Edmond Galabert. Calmann-Lévy, 1909

H. SUTHERLAND EDWARDS

The Prima Donna. Remington and Co., 1888

EDMOND GALABERT

Georges Bizet. Souvenirs et Correspondence. Calmann - Lévy. 1877

LOUIS GALLET

Notes d'un Librettiste. 1891

GUIDO M. GATTI

Giorgio Bizet.

CHARLES GUADIER

Carmen de Bizet. Etude historique et critique. Analyse Musicale. (Les Chefs-d'œuvre de la Musique). Mellotée.

HENRY GAUTHIER-VILLARS

Bizet. (Les Musiciens Célèbres). Henri Laurens.

HUGUES IMBERT

Portraits et Etudes. Lettres inédites de Georges Bizet. Fischbacher. 1894
Georges Bizet (Bibliothèque de l'art ancien et moderne). Ollendorff. 1899

PAUL LANDORMY	*Bizet.* (*Les Maîtres de la Musique*). Félix Alcan. 1924
A. MARMONTEL	*Symphonistes et Virtuoses.* Heugel 1881
J. MASSENET	*Mes Souvenirs*
LEOPOLDO MASTRIGLI	*Giorgio Bizet. La sua vita e le sue opere.* 1888
OVIDE MUSIN	*My Memories.* Musin Publishing Co., New York. 1920
CHARLES PIGOT	*Georges Bizet et son œuvre.* Dentu. 1886. New edn., Delagrave. 1911
ROMAIN ROLLAND	*Musicians of To-day.* Kegan Paul. 1915
OCTAVE SÉRÉ	*Musiciens français d'Aujourd'hui.* Mercure de France. 1915
JULIEN TIERSOT	*Un demi-siècle de Musique française* (1870–1919). (*Les Maîtres de la Musique*). Félix Alcan. 1918
ADOLF WEISSMANN	*Bizet* (*Die Musik*) Berlin
L'ART DU THÉÂTRE	January, 1905
LA REVUE THÉÂTRALE	January, 1905
LE THÉÂTRE	January, 1905
MUSICA	February, 1905, June, 1912, and July, 1912.

INDEX